T0126903

Mammals _of_ Michigan

Field Guide

by Stan Tekiela

Adventure Publications
Cambridge, Minnesota

To my wife, Katherine, and daughter, Abigail, with all my love

Acknowledgments

I would like to thank technical editor Sharon Jansa, Ph.D., Curator of Mammals at the Bell Museum of Natural History, and Assistant Professor of Ecology, Evolution and Behavior at the University of Minnesota, whose extensive knowledge of mammals significantly contributed to the accuracy of this book. A very special thanks to the following people and organizations, whose dedication to animals and animal expertise helped make this book possible.

Lee and Sandy Greenly, Minnesota Wildlife Connection (Sandstone) • Northern Trail Staff, Minnesota Zoo (Apple Valley) • Duluth Zoo (Duluth) • Ed Pitzenberger, Instructor, Environmental Education, Triton High School (Dodge Center) • "Trapper Phil" Philip A. Harry (Blaine) • Peggy Callahan, Executive Director, and Staff, Wildlife Science Center (Forest Lake) • Phil Jenni, Executive Director, and Staff, Wildlife Rehabilitation Center of Minnesota (Roseville) • Jil Ocel, Animal Productions, Inc. (Farmington) • Marv Roller (Fargo, ND) • Ben Sosniecki, Photographer (Chanhassen)

Edited by Sandy Livoti and Deborah Walsh

Cover and book design by Jonathan Norberg

Silhouettes, tracks and range maps by Anthony Hertzel

Photo credits by photographer and page number:

Cover photo: Fisher by Stan Tekiela
Mary Clay/DPA*: 171 **E. R. Degginger/DPA***: 6, 12, 30 **Dwight Kuhn**: 24, 27 (both) **Maslowski Wildlife Productions**: 4, 28, 38, 52, 134 (main), 156, 159 (winter), 164, 167, 170 **Gary Meszaros/DPA***: 11 (top), 18, 54 (inset), 70 (main), 71 **Skip Moody/DPA***: 31 **Philip Myers**: 20, 22, 64, 76 **Stan Osolinski/DPA***: 166 **James F. Parnell**: 11 (bottom), 40, 79, 158 **B. Moose Peterson/WRP***: 26 **Rod Planck/DPA***: 202 (winter) **Ann and Rob Simpson**: 15 **Merlin D. Tuttle/BCI***: 90 (main), 92, 94, 98 (main), 100, 102, 106 (main), 110 (main), 114, 116, 118, 119, 122 (main) **John and Gloria Tveten**: 7 (bottom), 54 (main), 66, 74 (main) **R. Wayne VanDevender**: 7 (top), 39, 42, 43, 78, 159 (bottom) **Jim Zipp**: 110 (male) **Stan Tekiela**: all other photos
*BCI: Bat Conservation International, Inc.; DPA: Dembinsky Photo Associates; WRP: Wildlife Research Photography

To the best of the publisher's knowledge, all photos were of live mammals. Some were photographed in a controlled condition.

15 14 13 12 11 10 9 8

Mammals of Michigan Field Guide
Copyright © 2005 by Stan Tekiela
Published by Adventure Publications, an imprint of AdventureKEEN
310 Garfield Street South
Cambridge, Minnesota 55008
(800) 678-7006
www.adventurepublications.net
All rights reserved
Printed in China
ISBN 978-1-59193-111-9 (pbk.)

TABLE OF CONTENTS

Introduction

The Mammals

MICHIGAN'S MAMMALS

Michigan is a great place for wildlife watchers! This state is one of the few places to see magnificent mammals such as the elusive Gray Wolf. We also have a small population of Canada Lynx. Bobcats and fleet-footed Snowshoe Hares make their homes in the coniferous forests of Michigan's Upper Peninsula, while flying squirrels and tree-climbing Gray Foxes are found in deciduous forests in various parts of the state. Michigan is well known for its large population of black morph Gray Squirrels. If you are really lucky, you might hear the yips and howls of Coyotes. No matter where you turn in Michigan, there is a wide variety of mammals to see and enjoy.

WHAT IS A MAMMAL?

The first mammals appeared in the late Triassic Period, about 200 million years ago. These ancient mammals were small, lacked diversity and looked nothing like our current-day mammals. During the following Jurassic Period, mammal size and diversity started to increase. Mammals generally started to appear more like today's mammals in the Cenozoic Era, which occurred after the mass extinction of dinosaurs, about 60 million years ago.

Today, modern mammals are a large group of animals that includes nearly 5,500 species around the world, with more than 400 species in North America. Here in Michigan, we have 66 species. Except for the House Mouse and Norway Rat, the mammals of Michigan are native to the state. They range from the tiny Least Shrew, which is no larger than a human thumb, to the extremely large and majestic Moose, which can grow to nearly 8 feet (2.4 m) tall and weigh up to 1,400 pounds (630 kg). Bats are able to do what no other mammals can–fly.

All mammals have some common traits or characteristics. Mammals have a backbone (vertebra) and are warm-blooded (endothermic). In endothermic animals, the process of eating and breaking down food in the digestive tract produces heat, which keeps the animal warm even on cold winter nights. Except during periods of hibernation or torpor, the body temperature of mammals stays within a narrow range, just as it does in people. Body temperature is controlled with rapid, open-mouthed breathing known as panting, by shunting blood flow to or away from areas with networks of blood vessels such as ears for cooling or to conserve heat. When blood flows through vessels that are close to the surface of skin, heat is released and the body is cooled. When blood flows away from the surface of skin, heat is conserved.

Most mammals are covered with a thick coat of fur or hair. Fur is critical for survival and needs to be kept clean and in good condition. Very few animals would be able to survive a Michigan winter without the amazing insulating qualities of fur. In some animals such as the Northern River Otter, the fur is so thick it keeps the underlying skin warm and dry even while swimming. Just as birds must preen their feathers to maintain good health, animals spend hours each day licking and "combing" or grooming their fur. You can easily observe this grooming behavior in your pet cat or dog.

Mammals share several other characteristics. All females bear live young and suckle their babies with milk produced from the mammary glands. Mother's milk provides young mammals with total nourishment during the first part of their lives. Also, mammals have sound-conducting bones in their middle ears. These bones give animals the ability to hear as humans do and, in many cases, hear much better.

Mammals are diphyodont, meaning they have two sets of teeth. There are milk or deciduous teeth, which fall out, and permanent teeth, also known as adult teeth. Adult teeth usually consist of incisors, canines, premolars and molars, but these categories can be highly variable in each mammal family. Teeth are often used to classify or group mammals into families in the same manner as the bill of a bird is used to classify or group birds into families.

Reproduction in mammals can be complex and difficult to understand. Many mammals have delayed implantation, which means after the egg and sperm have joined (impregnation), the resulting embryo remains in a suspended state until becoming implanted in the uterine wall. The delay time can be anywhere from a few days to weeks or months. An animal that becomes stressed from lack of food will pass the embryo out of the reproductive tract, and no pregnancy occurs. Conversely, well-fed mothers may have twins or even triplets. Bats and some other species store sperm in the reproductive tract over winter. Impregnation is delayed until spring, and implantation occurs right after impregnation. This process is known as delayed impregnation.

Most mammals are nocturnal, secretive and don't make a lot of noise, so they tend to go unnoticed. Signs of mammals such as tracks or scat are often more commonly seen than the actual animal. However, if you spend some time in the right habitat at the right time of day, your chances of seeing mammals will increase.

IDENTIFICATION STEP-BY-STEP

Fortunately, most large mammals are easy to identify and are not confused with other species. This is not the case, however, with small mammals such as mice or voles. Small animals, while plentiful, can be a challenge to correctly identify because they often have only minor differences in the teeth or internal organs and bones. Thus, every effort has been made to provide relevant identification information including range maps, which can help you eliminate some choices.

This field guide is organized by families, starting with small animals such as shrews and mice, and ending with large mammals such as bear and bison. Within each family section, the animals are in size order from small to large.

Each mammal has four pages of color photos and text, with a silhouette of the animal illustrated on the first description page. Each silhouette is located in a quick-compare tab in the upper right corner. Decide which animal group you are seeing, use the quick-compare tabs to locate the pages for that group, then compare the photos with your animal. If you aren't sure of the identity, the text on description pages explains identifying features that may or may not be easily seen. The first description page for each species also has a compare section with notes about similar species in this field guide. Other pertinent details and the naturalist facts in Stan's Notes will help you correctly identify your mammal in question.

Of course, if you already know the name of your animal, simply use the index to quickly find the page and learn more about the species from the text and photos.

For many people, an animal's track or silhouette is all they might see of an animal. However, tracks in mud or snow and silhouettes are often difficult to identify. Special quick-compare pages, beginning on pg. xii, are a great place to start the identification process. These pages group similar kinds of animals and tracks side by side for easy comparison. For example, all hoofed animals such as deer and bison are grouped in one section and all doglike animals are grouped in another. Within the groupings, silhouettes and tracks are illustrated in relative size from small to large. This format allows you to compare one silhouette or track shape and size with another that is similarly shaped and sized. When you don't know whether you're seeing the silhouette or track of a coyote or wolf, a deer or elk or other similar species, use the quick-compare pages for quick and easy reference.

To begin, find the group that your unknown silhouette or track looks similar to and start comparing. Since each group has relatively few animals, it won't take long to narrow your choices. A ruler can be handy to measure your track and compare it with the size given in the book. To confirm the identity of the silhouette or track and for more detailed information about the animal, refer to the description pages for the number of toes, length of stride and other distinguishing characteristics.

TAXONOMY OF MICHIGAN'S MAMMALS

Biologists have classified mammals based on ancestry and physical characteristics. Michigan's mammals are grouped into seven scientific orders. Charts with the scientific classification (taxonomy) are shown on Appendix pages 270-279. Each of the seven charts starts with one of the orders and shows all of the scientific families and mammals in that particular order.

CAUTION

All mammals except for the House Mouse and the Norway Rat are protected and regulated in Michigan. Hunting, trapping, possessing and other activities involving animals are regulated by the Michigan Department of Natural Resources (DNR). You should familiarize yourself with the laws and seasons before any kill trapping, live trapping and hunting.

As interesting as all of these animals are, resist any temptation to capture any animal for a pet. Wild animals, even babies, never make good pets. Wild animals often have specific dietary and habitat requirements that rarely can be duplicated in a captive situation, and many will not survive. In many cases, capturing animals for pets is also illegal. This practice not only diminishes the population, it reduces the possibility for future reproduction. Furthermore, some animals are uncommon in Michigan, and their populations can be even more quickly depleted.

Live trapping of animals in an attempt to rid your yard of them rarely works. The removal of an animal from its habitat creates a void that is quickly filled with a neighboring animal or its offspring, recreating the original situation. Moreover, an unfortunate animal that is live trapped and moved to a new location often cannot find a habitat with an adequate food supply, shelter or a territory that is not already occupied. Animals that have been moved often die from exposure to weather, are struck by vehicles while crossing roads or are killed by resident animals. With habitat ranges growing smaller every year, removing just one animal can have a direct impact on the local population of a species. We can all learn to live with our wild animals with just a few modifications to our yards and attitudes. Observe and record animals with your camera, but leave them where they belong–in the wild.

Encounters with wildlife often involve injured or orphaned animals. Many well-intentioned people with little or no resources or knowledge of what is needed try to care for such animals. Injured or orphaned animals deserve the best care, so please do the right thing if you find one and turn it over to a licensed professional wildlife rehabilitator. Information about wildlife rehabilitation in Michigan is listed in the resource section of this field guide. The rehabilitation staff may often be able to give you updates on the condition of an animal you bring in and even when it is released. When you take an animal to a rehab center, you might also want to consider making a monetary donation to help cover the costs involved for its care.

Enjoy the Mammals!

Stan

Body length measurements
do not include tail.

Average size of the smallest and
largest of this group compared to
an 8" hand.

Silhouettes are in proportion by
average body length. Tracks are in
proportion by average largest
foot. Front track is on the left and
hind is on the right.

1¾"

Least Shrew pg. 5

⅛" ⅜"

2"

Masked Shrew pg. 9

⅛" ⅜"

3½"

Northern Short-tailed
Shrew pg. 17

⅜" ⅝"

3½"

Woodland Jumping
Mouse pg. 41

½" 1¼"

4⅛"

Woodland Vole pg. 65

¼" ⅝"

4½"

Arctic Shrew pg. 21

⅛" ⅜"

5"

Star-nosed Mole pg. 29

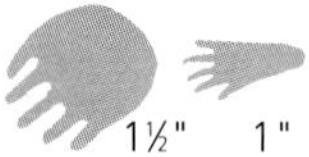

1½" 1"

5¼"

Southern Bog Lemmin
pg. 77

⅝" ¾"

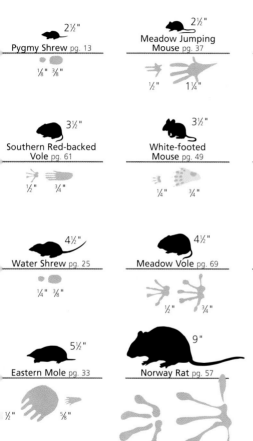

Pygmy Shrew pg. 13 — 2½"
⅛" ⅜"

Meadow Jumping Mouse pg. 37 — 2½"
½" 1¼"

House Mouse pg. 45 — 3¼"
¼" ½"

Southern Red-backed Vole pg. 61 — 3½"
½" ¾"

White-footed Mouse pg. 49 — 3½"
¼" ¾"

Deer Mouse pg. 53 — 3¾"
¼" ¾"

Water Shrew pg. 25 — 4½"
¼" ⅜"

Meadow Vole pg. 69 — 4½"
½" ¾"

Prairie Vole pg. 73 — 4½"
½" ⅞"

Eastern Mole pg. 33 — 5½"
½" ⅝"

Norway Rat pg. 57 — 9"
1" 1½"

Body length measurements
do not include tail.

Average size of the smallest and largest of this group compared to a 6' human.

Silhouettes are in proportion by average body length. Tracks are in proportion by average largest foot. Front track is on the left and hind is on the right.

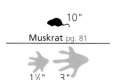

10"

Muskrat pg. 81

1½" 3"

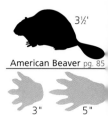

3½'

American Beaver pg. 85

3" 5"

Body length measurements
do not include tail.

Average size of the smallest and largest of this group compared to an 8" hand.

Silhouettes are in proportion to each other by average body length. Average wingspan (W) is on the left.

W 9" 1¾"

Little Brown Bat
pg. 89

no tracks

W 9" 2⅛"

Eastern Pipistrelle
pg. 93

no tracks

W 13½" 2½"

Red Bat pg. 109

no tracks

W 13½" 2½"

Silver-haired Bat pg. 113

no tracks

W 9"  2¼"

Northern Myotis
pg. 97
no tracks

W 13½"  2¼"

Evening Bat pg. 101
no tracks

W 13½"  2½"

Big Brown Bat pg. 105
no tracks

W 9"  2¾"

Indiana Bat pg. 117
no tracks

W 15½"  3"

Hoary Bat pg. 121
no tracks

Body length measurements
do not include tail.

Average size of the smallest and
largest of this group compared to
a 6' human.

Silhouettes are in proportion by
average body length. Tracks are in
proportion by average largest
foot. Front track is on the left and
hind is on the right.

4½"

Least Chipmunk pg. 125

½" 1"

6"

Southern Flying Squirrel
pg. 133

½" 1"

8"

Red Squirrel pg. 141

¾" 1½"

9½"

Eastern Gray Squirrel
pg. 145

1" 2¼"

Eastern Chipmunk
pg. 129

⅝" 1⅜"

7"

Thirteen-lined Ground Squirrel pg. 137

1" 1½"

8"

Northern Flying Squirrel
pg. 133

¾" 1½"

12½"

Eastern Fox Squirrel
pg. 149

1½" 2⅞"

23"

Woodchuck pg. 153

3¼" 3⅜"

Body length measurements
do not include tail.

Average size of the smallest and
largest of this group compared to
a 6' human.

Silhouettes are in proportion by
average body length. Tracks are in
proportion by average largest
foot. Front track is on the left and
hind is on the right.

6½"
Least Weasel pg. 157
½" ½"

8½"
Short-tailed Weasel
pg. 161
¾" ⅞"

22"
Fisher pg. 177
2½" 2½"

22"
Striped Skunk pg. 193
1⅜" 2¾"

12"

Long-tailed Weasel
pg. 165

¾" ⅞"

16½"

American Marten pg. 169

1½"   1⅝"

17"

Mink pg. 173

1½"   2⅝"

25"

American Badger pg. 181

2"   2"

30½"

Wolverine pg. 185

5"   5"

36"

Northern River Otter
pg. 189

3⅜"   3½"

Body length measurements
do not include tail.

Average size of the smallest and
largest of this group compared to
a 6' human.

16"

Eastern Cottontail
pg. 197

1" 3½"

17½"

Snowshoe Hare pg. 201

1" 4½"

Body length measurements
do not include tail.

Average size of the smallest and
largest of this group compared to
a 6' human.

23"

North American
Porcupine pg. 205

2¼" 3¼"

24½"

Northern Raccoon
pg. 209

2¾" 4"

Silhouettes are in proportion by
average body length. Tracks are in
proportion by average largest
foot. Front track is on the left and
hind is on the right.

27½"

rginia Opossum pg. 213

1½"   2"

Body length measurements
do not include tail.

Average size of the smallest and
largest of this group compared to
a 6' human.

23"
Gray Fox pg. 217
1½" 1⅜"

23"
Red Fox pg. 221
2" 1⅞"

Body length measurements
do not include tail.

Average size of the smallest and
largest of this group compared to
a 6' human.

3'
Bobcat pg. 233
2" 2"

3¼"
Canada Lynx pg. 237
3½" 3½"

Silhouettes are in proportion by
average body length. Tracks are in
proportion by average largest
foot. Front track is on the left and
hind is on the right.

Coyote pg. 225

2¼ " 2⅛ "

Gray Wolf pg. 229

6 " 5⅞ "

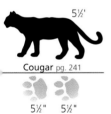

Cougar pg. 241

5½ " 5½ "

Body length measurements
do not include tail.

Average size of the smallest and
largest of this group compared to
a 6' human.

White-tailed Deer pg. 245

5½'

2½"   2⅜"

8'

Moose pg. 249

5½"   5¾"

Body length measurements
do not include tail.

Average size of the smallest and
largest of this group compared to
a 6' human.

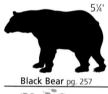

5¼'

Black Bear pg. 257

4"   8"

Silhouettes are in proportion by
average body length. Tracks are in
proportion by average largest
foot. Front track is on the left and
hind is on the right.

8¼'

10'

Elk pg. 253

4¼" 4⅛"

American Bison pg. 261

6½" 6⅜"

Common Name

Scientific name

Family: common family name (scientific family name)

Size: (L) average length or range of length of body from head to rump; (T) average length or range of length of tail; (H) average height or range of height to top of back; (W) average wingspan

Weight: average weight or range of weight, may include (M) male and (F) female weights

Description: brief description of the mammal, may include color morphs, seasonal variations or differences between male and female

Origin/Age: native or non-native to Michigan; average life span in the wild

Compare: notes about other species that look similar and the pages on which they can be found, may include extra information to help identify

Habitat: environment where the animal is found (e.g., forests, prairies, wetlands)

Home: description of nest, burrow or den; may include other related information

Food: herbivore, carnivore, insectivore, omnivore; what the animal eats most of the time; may include other related information

Sounds: vocalization or other noises the animal creates; may include variant sounds or other information

Breeding: mating season; length of gestation; may include additional comments

Young: number of offspring born per year and when; may include description or birth weight

1

summer coat

winter coat

silver morph | black morph

scat

Signs: evidence that the animal was there or is near; may include a description of scat; other comments

Activity: diurnal, nocturnal, crepuscular; other comments

Tracks: forepaw and hind paw or hoof size and shape, largest size first; pattern of tracks; description of prints, may include stride; other comments

Tracks and Pattern

Stan's Notes: Interesting gee-whiz natural history information. This can be something to look or listen for, or something to help positively identify the animal such as remarkable features. May include additional photos to illustrate juveniles, nests, unique behaviors and other key characteristics.

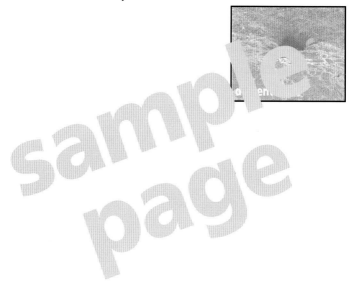

kits

3

Least Shrew
Cryptotis parva

Family: Shrews (Soricidae)

Size: L 1½-2¼" (4-5.5 cm); T ½-¾" (1-2 cm)

Weight: ¼ oz. (7 g)

Description: Mostly brown above, but fur can be gray. Lighter belly. Pointed snout. Tiny dark eyes. Short tail, never more than twice as long as the hind paws. Small pink feet. Ears barely visible.

Origin/Age: native; 1-2 years

Compare: Smaller than the Masked Shrew (pg. 9), which has a longer snout and tail. The more common Northern Short-tailed Shrew (pg. 17) is much larger and darker overall. One of the few shrews with a tail length that is less than half the length of its body.

Habitat: fields, wetlands, meadows, shrubby areas

Home: nest made of dried leaves and grasses, frequently well hidden on the ground

Food: insectivore, carnivore; beetles, crickets, spiders, grasshoppers, slugs, earthworms, snails

Sounds: inconsequential; sharp squeaks and high-pitched whistles can be heard from a distance up to 2 feet (61 cm)

Breeding: Mar-Nov mating; 21-23 days gestation

Young: 1-6 offspring several times per year; born naked with eyes closed, weaned at about 3 weeks

(more information on next page)

Signs: partially eaten insects near the nest; extremely tiny, dark scat, widely scattered

Activity: nocturnal, diurnal to a much lesser degree; may be more active during the day in summer, when nights are shorter

Tracks: hind paw ¼-½" (.6-1 cm) long, forepaw slightly smaller; 1 set of 4 tracks, but prints are so close together they appear as 1 track; 4 prints together are 1 square inch (6.4 sq. cm), often lacks a tail drag mark due to its short tail

Stan's Notes: One of Michigan's smallest and least studied shrew species, thus not much is known about its biology or range in the state. Range in the U.S. is widespread from Minnesota to Texas to Florida and up the entire East coast, excluding New England.

Sometimes called Bee Shrew because it supposedly lives in beehives; however, this has never been studied or widely reported and may be a reference to the animal's small size.

Hunts for invertebrates by probing through leaf litter with its nose, smelling for prey. Often feeds only on the internal organs of large insects. Subdues prey by capturing and biting off the head, which makes it easier to get to internal organs. Like other shrews, it eats nearly its own body weight in food each day.

While most other shrews species are solitary, the Least Shrew is apparently more social, with many individuals in one nest. It is thought that owls are the major predators of the Least Shrew.

Masked Shrew
Sorex cinereus

Family: Shrews (Soricidae)

Size: L 1¾-2¼" (4.5-5.5 cm); T 1-2" (2.5-5 cm)

Weight: ¼ oz. (7 g)

Description: Overall brown to gray with lighter gray-to-white belly. A very long, pointed snout. Tiny dark eyes. Ears slightly visible. Long hairy tail, brown above and lighter below with a dark tuft at tip.

Origin/Age: native; 1-2 years

Compare: The small size, brown color and long tail of the Masked Shrew help distinguish it from the other shrews in Michigan. Pygmy Shrew (pg. 13) is slightly larger. Use the ranges to help identify.

Habitat: farmlands, prairies, fields, bogs, wetlands, moist deciduous forests

Home: nest, 4-6 inches (10-15 cm) wide, made of leaves and grasses, under a log or rock

Food: insectivore, carnivore; insects, ants, slugs, spiders, earthworms, small mammals such as mice

Sounds: inconsequential; sharp squeaks and high-pitched whistles

Breeding: spring to autumn mating; 18 days gestation

Young: 5-7 offspring 2-3 times per year; young are born naked with eyes closed, eyes open at 17-19 days, weaned at about 20 days, on own within days of being weaned, young born in fall are less likely to survive due to lack of food

(more information on next page) 9

Signs: tiny tunnels or runways in freshly dug soil; shrew is rarely, if ever, seen

Activity: diurnal, nocturnal; active under snow in winter

Tracks: hind paw ¼-½" (.6-1 cm) long, forepaw slightly smaller; 1 set of 4 tracks, but prints are so close together they appear as 1 track; 4 prints together are 1 square inch (6.4 sq. cm), sometimes has a slight tail drag mark

Stan's Notes: This very secretive, solitary animal is rarely seen because of its underground lifestyle. Also called Cinereus Shrew, it is one of the smallest mammals in Michigan. It is also one of the most widespread mammals in North America, ranging all across Canada and Alaska and the northern-tiered states.

Its long pointed snout is characteristic of all 33 species of shrews seen in North America. Gives off a strong musky odor, which makes it unattractive to large mammalian predators, but the scent does not seem to deter birds of prey such as owls and hawks. Heart rate will race to as many as 1,200 beats per minute when it is excited. Can die from fright when captured.

Has little body mass due to its small size, so it must feed nearly every hour to keep warm or starve to death. Moves constantly, darting about to find food. Often eats more than its own body weight daily in worms, slugs and beetles. Will kill mice, which are larger than itself. Seeks dormant insects and larvae in winter. Does not hibernate.

A desirable animal to have around your home and yard because it eats many harmful insects and keeps populations of mice in check. Does not transmit rabies and is not harmful to humans.

Pygmy Shrew
Sorex hoyi

Family: Shrews (Soricidae)

Size: L 2-3" (5-7.5 cm); T 1" (2.5 cm)

Weight: ⅛ oz. (4 g)

Description: Brown to gray above, sometimes coppery brown. Belly is light gray to silver. Long pointed snout. Ears hidden by fur. Tiny dark eyes. A long hairy tail, dark brown above and paler below, about 40-50 percent of total length.

Origin/Age: native; 1 year

Compare: Northern Short-tailed Shrew (pg. 17) is larger, much darker and has a shorter tail. Consider the range and rarity when identifying this species.

Habitat: coniferous forests, sphagnum moss bogs, brushy fields

Home: nest made from dried plant material, 2 openings, under a log or stump; builds several nests

Food: insectivore, carnivore; beetles, crickets, small grasshoppers, spiders, worms, small amphibians

Sounds: inconsequential; sharp squeaks and high-pitched whistles

Breeding: Mar-Sep mating; 18-20 days gestation; breeds less often in northern parts of Michigan

Young: 2-8 offspring 1-2 times per year; born naked with eyes closed

(more information on next page)

Signs: multiple round nests made of plant material with surface runways leading to and from nests

Activity: nocturnal, diurnal; slightly more active at night

Tracks: hind paw ⅜" (.9 cm) long, forepaw slightly smaller; 1 set of 4 tracks, but prints are so close together they appear as 1 track; 4 prints together are 1 square inch (6.4 sq. cm), sometimes has a tail drag mark

Stan's Notes: This is one of the smallest and rarest mammals in Michigan and North America, never found in great abundance. Known to inhabit only those areas where coniferous trees are most plentiful. Its range extends from New England to Michigan, Wisconsin, Minnesota and west across Canada to Alaska.

Tolerates a wide variety of habitats from wet to dry and cold to warm, regardless of the vegetative type. Usually associated with a specific vegetative variety including trees such as Paper Birch, Jack Pine, hazelnut, aspen and alder.

Not much is known about the Pygmy Shrew. Runs with quick spurts, often holding tail slightly curved. Frequently stands on hind feet in kangaroo fashion. An excellent climber and is able to jump several inches into the air. Presumably uses its sense of smell to hunt for small insect prey in leaf litter. Also feeds on limited amounts of plant material.

Northern Short-tailed Shrew
Blarina brevicauda

Family: Shrews (Soricidae)

Size: L 3-4" (7.5-10 cm); T ¾-1" (2-2.5 cm)

Weight: ½-1 oz. (14-28 g)

Description: Overall dark to slate gray (younger shrews often darker). Long pointed snout. Small pink feet. Short, nearly naked tail. Tiny dark eyes, often not noticed. Ears barely visible.

Origin/Age: native; 1-2 years

Compare: Much larger than Masked Shrew (pg. 9), which has a longer, narrower snout and a longer tail. Much more common than Least Shrew (pg. 5), which is smaller, grayer and found only in southern Michigan. Pygmy Shrew (pg. 13) is smaller, light brown and has a longer tail.

Habitat: wide variety of habitats such as moist deciduous woodlands, coniferous forests, fields, meadows, yards and gardens

Home: bulky nest, 6-10 inches (15-25 cm) wide, made from dried grasses and leaves, usually beneath a log or rock or inside a rotting stump

Food: insectivore, carnivore; beetles, earthworms, snails, spiders, mice, voles, toads, subterranean fungi

Sounds: inconsequential; sharp squeaks and high-pitched whistles can be heard from a distance up to 10 feet (3 m)

Breeding: Apr-Aug mating; 21-22 days gestation

Young: 4-7 offspring once per year; born only as large as a honeybee and naked with eyes closed, weaned after about 2 days

(more information on next page) 17

Signs: well-worn inch-wide runways or tunnels through grass or snow, partially eaten mice and toads, piles of snail shells and insect parts under a log, fallen tree bark or other shelter

Activity: diurnal, nocturnal; active year-round

Tracks: hind paw ½-¾" (1-2 cm) long, forepaw slightly smaller; continuous grooves in snow or runways in lawns with no distinct prints; continuous grooves and runways are due to its low-slung body and short legs, which do not allow it to hop or jump

Stan's Notes: One of the largest and most widespread shrews in Michigan. At times it can be the most abundant small mammal in the state and North America. Populations can climb to very high levels and then drop suddenly, making it seem like it is everywhere one year and nonexistent the next.

Unique because it is one of only two North American mammals that produces a poisonous saliva. It cannot inject the poison, but chews it into a wound. The poison paralyzes small prey such as mice; can cause tingling and numbness in people.

A solitary shrew. Excavates tunnels underground or runways just below leaf litter, where it patrols for food. Ears and eyes function, but usually go unnoticed because they are so small. Finds most of its prey by smell and feel. Uses ultrasonic clicks (echolocation) to detect objects in dark tunnels, much like a bat. Hunts for short periods of 3-5 minutes, then rests for 20-30 minutes. Consumes half its own weight in food every day. Caches food underground, returning often to eat and replenish the supply.

Many cannot live more than 48 hours in captivity without food and water. Its large size enables this shrew to conserve heat and live longer without food than the other shrews. Smaller shrews cannot live more than 24 hours without food and water.

The male will scent mark its territory with urine, feces or oily secretions from glands near the base of the tail. Marking territory helps reduce the chance of a fatal encounter since rival neighbors will sometimes fight each other to death. Scent marking also advertises social status, helps to attract mates and, as an added benefit, may deter predators that find the glands distasteful.

The female is ready to reproduce as early as 46 days. Mates may stay together for long periods, maybe even for life.

Arctic Shrew
Sorex arcticus

Family: Shrews (Soricidae)

Size: L 4-5" (10-13 cm); T 1-1¾" (2.5-4.5 cm)

Weight: ¼ oz. (7 g)

Description: Brown back with lighter brown sides and gray belly. Tricolored body distinctive in adults, not in juveniles. Long pointed snout. Tiny dark eyes. Long hairy tail, brown above, paler below. Ears barely visible. Male slightly larger than female.

Origin/Age: native; 1-2 years

Compare: Much larger than the Masked Shrew (pg. 9) and Pygmy Shrew (pg. 13). Smaller than the Water Shrew (pg. 25), which has an aquatic lifestyle. Like other shrew species, its tiny eyes and ears distinguish it from mice.

Habitat: wetlands, bogs, marshes, sedge meadows, coniferous forests, tundra

Home: bulky nest, 6-10 inches (15-25 cm) wide, made of dried grasses and leaves, usually underneath a log or rock or inside a rotting stump; female will build a new, larger nest a couple days before she gives birth

Food: insectivore; beetle larvae, beetles, centipedes, caterpillars, ants

Sounds: inconsequential; sharp squeaks and high-pitched whistles, gives a low, rapid chittering noise when disturbed

Breeding: Mar-Oct mating; 24-27 days gestation

Young: 6-8 offspring up to 3 times per year; born naked with eyes closed, weaned at 18-24 days

(more information on next page) 21

Signs: aboveground inch-wide runways, underground tunnels leading in and out of mounds in the ground

Activity: mainly nocturnal, diurnal; active during the day with frequent rest periods

Tracks: hind paw ¼-½" (.6-1 cm) long, forepaw slightly smaller; 1 set of 4 tracks, but prints are so close together they appear as 1 track; 4 prints together are 1 square inch (6.4 sq. cm), sometimes has a slight tail drag mark

Stan's Notes: It is often difficult to identify a shrew to a specific species without a very close examination of its teeth. The most distinctive characteristic of the Arctic Shrew is its tricolored body, which is more obvious in adults in late summer and winter. This unique coloration is the basis for its other common names, Saddle-backed Shrew or Black-backed Shrew.

More common across Canada, with the southernmost part of its range dipping into Michigan. Often not associated with people, preferring natural environments without human development. Also prefers open habitats as opposed to forests.

Observations of its hunting behavior suggest it uses vision to find prey and support that it is one of the few shrew species with acute vision. In addition to having a short life span, it is estimated that 1 in 7 individuals die within the first month of life. Nearly 80 percent die before reaching sexual maturity.

Female becomes sexually mature at 4-5 months. When a female is born early in the year, she can bear young during the same breeding season; however, most females breed the following year. A female often mates within days after she weans her young. The male does not take part in raising young.

Water Shrew
Sorex palustris

Family: Shrews (Soricidae)

Size: L 4-5" (10-13 cm); T 2-3" (5-7.5 cm)

Weight: ½ oz. (14 g)

Description: Overall dark brown to black with a bright white belly. Long pointed snout. Tiny dark eyes. Fringe of stiff hairs on back of feet. Very long tail, nearly half its total length. Ears not visible.

Origin/Age: native; 3-5 years

Compare: Long pointed snout like the other shrews, but its extremely long tail and the aquatic lifestyle make it easy to differentiate. The distinctive black body and white belly also help to identify.

Habitat: lakes, bogs, streams, ponds

Home: bulky nest, 6-10 inches (15-25 cm) wide, made of dried grasses and leaves, usually in or near a sphagnum bog mound, beneath a fallen log or inside a rotting stump

Food: insectivore, carnivore; aquatic insects, spiders, slugs, earthworms, leeches, small fish

Sounds: inconsequential; sharp squeaks and high-pitched whistles

Breeding: Jan-Aug mating; 21 days gestation

Young: 5-8 offspring up to 3 times per year; born naked with eyes closed, young do not enter water until they are fully furred

(more information on next page)

Signs: splashing at the edge of water during the night, small runways in moss along the banks of lakes and streams

Activity: nocturnal, diurnal; most active after dark (especially in summer), usually not seen in the winter

Tracks: hind paw ¼-½" (.6-1 cm) long, forepaw slightly smaller; 1 set of 4 tracks, but prints are so close together they appear as 1 track; 4 prints together are 1 square inch (6.4 sq. cm), has a tail drag mark leading in or out of open water or in snow, lacking a tail drag mark in mud during warm weather

Stan's Notes: One of the largest shrews in Michigan. As the name implies, it lives near or in the water.

This shrew can actually run across the surface of calm water, thanks to the fringe of hairs on its hind feet, which trap oxygen and increase the surface area. Splashing sounds made while it runs can often be heard at night, but the animal moves so quickly it is hard to spot with a flashlight. The hairs also act like fins, aiding underwater swimming. The  shrew uses these hairs like a comb to help remove water from its velvety fur, which is water resistant and dries very quickly.

Air trapped in the fur helps the Water Shrew to surface rapidly after diving to the bottom of lakes, streams or bogs or, when it stops swimming, to pop to the surface like a cork.

fringe of hairs

The female may not reproduce until her second year. A mother Water Shrew has only six teats. If she has more than six young, those unable to nurse will most certainly die due to their nearly constant need to feed.

27

Star-nosed Mole
Condylura cristata

Family: Moles (Talpidae)

Size: L 3-7" (7.5-18 cm); T ¾-1¼" (2-3 cm)

Weight: 1-2½ oz. (28-71 g)

Description: Fur is dark gray to nearly black. Twenty or more thin, fleshy pink projections on nose in a circular pattern. Short legs. Extremely large front feet with long, well-defined claws. A long tail with sparse hair, constricted at base. Invisible ears. Pinpoint eyes, often hidden.

Origin/Age: native; 1-2 years

Compare: Spends more of its time above ground than the Eastern Mole (pg. 33). Look for large, fleshy pink projections on the nose to help identify.

Habitat: wet woodlands, moist fields, wetlands, ponds, lakes, streams

Home: burrow, beneath a log or fallen tree, nest is lined with dead leaves and grasses during summer, in a chamber connected to a tunnel system below the frost line during winter, separate chambers for giving birth and raising young

Food: insectivore, carnivore; insects, slugs, earthworms, crustaceans, fish

Sounds: inconsequential; rarely, if ever, heard

Breeding: Apr-May mating; 35-45 days gestation; starts to breed at 10 months

Young: 3-7 (average 5) offspring once per year in April or May with some born as late as August; born naked, helpless, with the "star" nose enclosed in a thin translucent membrane and eyes closed

(more information on next page) 29

Signs: ridges as a result of tunneling near the surface of soil, mounds of fresh soil (molehills) pushed up during construction of tunnels, runways on the surface leading to and from holes in the ground

Activity: diurnal, nocturnal; active year-round, spends less time underground than other moles

Tracks: hind paw 1" (2.5 cm) long with 5 toes, forepaw 1½" (4 cm) long with 5 toes; individual tracks are indistinguishable and create a single groove with claw marks, sometimes has a tail drag mark

Stan's Notes: This mole is one of the most recognizable small mammals in Michigan. Its fleshy, tentacle-like pink nose and long tail make it easy to identify. Nose projections (nasal rays) are presumably used to feel for worms in the darkness underground. Recent studies have indicated they contain highly sensitive tactile organs called Eimer's organs, believed to detect electrical fields given by prey. It is also thought that nasal rays help a mole manipulate objects such as food during capturing and eating. The tail fattens during spring and summer, presumably as an energy store for the breeding season and coming winter, thickening as a result of fat deposition. Main prey of this mole are earthworms and insects.

Eyes are very small and probably useful only to detect light. Digs less powerfully than the more common Eastern Mole, but is a very good swimmer. Able to dive after aquatic animals including fish. Propels itself underwater by moving its feet and tail for extra propulsion. Also a good tunneler, with tunnels often opening out underwater. Has additional paths or "runs" above ground.

Often gregarious and even colonial. Active under snow and even beneath the ice of frozen lakes and streams. Babies grow quickly, leaving nests and mothers at 3-4 weeks.

The genus name *Condylura* is Greek and means "knobby tail," referring to one of the first and, unfortunately, inaccurate drawings of this animal showing a bumpy or knobby tail, much like a string of beads. The species name *cristata* is Latin for "crest" or "tuft" and refers to the star-shaped pattern of projections on the nose. There are six other mole species north of Mexico in North America.

Eastern Mole
Scalopus aquaticus

Family: Moles (Talpidae)

Size: L 4-7" (10-18 cm); T ¾-1¼" (2-3 cm)

Weight: 3-5 oz. (85-142 g)

Description: Short silky fur, dark brown to gray with a silver sheen. Long pointed snout. Very large, naked front feet, more wide than long and resembling human hands with palms turned outward. Very short, nearly naked tail. Pinpoint eyes, frequently hidden by fur. Male slightly larger than female.

Origin/Age: native; 1-2 years

Compare: The largest mole species in Michigan, common in the Lower Peninsula. Slightly larger than the Star-nosed Mole (pg. 29) and lacks the large, obvious fleshy projections on its snout.

Habitat: dry grassy areas, fields, lawns, gardens, loose well-drained soils

Home: burrow, tunnels usually 4-20 inches (10-50 cm) belowground in summer, deeper tunnels below the frost line during winter, nest is in a chamber connected to a tunnel, with separate chambers for giving birth and raising young

Food: insectivore, herbivore; insects, grubs, roots, earthworms

Sounds: inconsequential; rarely, if ever, heard

Breeding: Feb-Mar mating; 32-42 days gestation

Young: 2-6 offspring once per year in early spring; born naked with eyes closed, weaned at 30-40 days, leaves nest chamber when weaned

(more information on next page) 33

tail

Signs: ridges of soil from tunnel construction just below the surface of the ground, sometimes small piles of soil on the ground (molehills) from digging deeper permanent tunnels

Activity: diurnal, nocturnal; active year-round, does not appear to time its activities with the rising and setting of the sun

Tracks: hind paw ⅝" (1.5 cm) long with 5 toes, forepaw 1½" (4 cm) long with 5 toes; individual tracks are indistinguishable and create a single groove with claw marks, sometimes has a tail drag mark; spends almost all of its time in its underground tunnel system, so tracks are rarely seen

Stan's Notes: The first time this animal was described in records was when a drowned mole was found in a well. It was presumed, in error, to be aquatic; hence the Latin species name *aquaticus*, which also refers to the slight webbing between its toes. This is the most subterranean mammal in Michigan, spending 99 percent of its life underground. Also called Common Mole or just Mole.

The Eastern Mole has no external ears. Its tiny eyes are covered with skin and detect light only, not shapes or colors. It has large white teeth, unlike the shrews, which have chestnut or tan teeth. Uses its very sensitive, flexible snout to find food by smelling and sensing vibrations with its whiskers. The nap of its short fur can lie forward or backward, making it easier to travel in either direction in tight tunnels. A narrow pelvis allows it to somersault often and reverse its heading.

Excavates its own tunnel system. Uses its front feet to dig while pushing loosened soil back and out of the way with its hind feet. Able to dig 1 foot (30 cm) per minute in loose soil. Digging and tunneling is beneficial to the environment; it aerates the soil and allows moisture to penetrate deeper into the ground.

Searches for food such as subterranean insects, earthworms and some plant roots in temporary tunnels, usually located just below the surface of the ground. Deeper permanent tunnels are used for living, nesting and depositing waste. Will move to even deeper tunnels below the frost line during winter.

The male will seek out a female in her tunnel to mate during late winter. It is thought that a female rarely leaves her tunnel system, except when a young female leaves the tunnels of her mother to establish her own.

Unlike most other small mammals, it reproduces only once each year. Not preyed upon as heavily due to its burrowing (fossorial) life, so does not need to reproduce often.

Meadow Jumping Mouse
Zapus hudsonius

Family: Jumping Mice (Dipodidae)

Size: L 2-3" (5-7.5 cm); T 4-6" (10-15 cm)

Weight: ¾-1 oz. (21-28 g)

Description: A reddish brown back with lighter brown sides. May have a dark stripe down the center of back. White belly hair. Large round ears. Prominent dark eyes. Long snout. Extremely long tail, dark above and white below.

Origin/Age: native; 1-2 years

Compare: Smaller overall with a shorter tail than Woodland Jumping Mouse (pg. 41) and lacks the distinctive tricolored body. The Woodland Jumping Mouse is found in coniferous forests in northern parts of Michigan, while the Meadow Jumping Mouse is seen in open regions throughout the state. Other mouse species have belly hair that is gray at the base and don't have tails as long as jumping mice.

Habitat: semi-woodlands, moist open fields

Home: nest made from dried grass, under a fallen log or clump of grass; used for hibernation

Food: herbivore, insectivore; underground fungi, seeds, fruit, insects

Sounds: inconsequential; scratching or scampering can be heard, drums front feet on ground if threatened

Breeding: May-Jul mating; 17-21 days gestation; will mate shortly after emerging from hibernation

Young: 4-7 pups twice per year; born naked with eyes closed

(more information on next page)

Signs: surface runways leading in many directions, grasses with missing seed heads (topped), piles of grass stems that are the same length and have seed heads removed

Activity: nocturnal; active 5-6 months of the year, hibernating from October to April or May

Tracks: hind paw 1¼" (3 cm) long with a long narrow heel and 5 toes, forepaw ½" (1 cm) long with 4 toes; 1 set of 4 tracks; tracks seen only in mud during months of activity

Stan's Notes: The jumping mouse got its name from its ability to leap up to 3 feet (1 m) to escape predators or when it is startled. Although the name implies that it jumps to get around, it usually walks on all four feet or moves in a series of small jumps.

Often will remain motionless after jumping several times. Uses its long tail, which is more than 50 percent of its total length, for balance while jumping. Hind legs are longer than front legs and are very fragile, often breaking when live-trapped for research.

Feeds during the summer on an underground fungus called *Endogone*, which it finds by smell. Does not store any food for winter, feeding heavily instead during the last month before it hibernates. Will gain up to 100 percent of its body weight in fat. It is a true hibernator, not active in winter. Male emerges from hibernation in April, female a couple weeks later. Some studies show that many apparently do not survive the winter, as only half the population appears the following spring.

Matures sexually before reaching 1 year of age. Many females that were born in springtime are breeding in July. Reproduces twice each year.

This mouse does not cause crop damage and will rarely enter a dwelling. Jumping mice (genera *Zapus* and *Napaeozapus*) are found only in North America.

Woodland Jumping Mouse
Napaeozapus insignis

Family: Jumping Mice (Dipodidae)

Size: L 3-4" (7.5-10 cm); T 4-7" (10-18 cm)

Weight: ¼-1 oz. (21-28 g)

Description: A distinctly tricolored body. Back is brown, sides are orange or yellow to light brown and belly is white. Large round ears. Prominent dark eyes. A long snout. Extremely long tail, dark above and white below, usually with a white tip.

Origin/Age: native; 1-2 years

Compare: Similar to the Meadow Jumping Mouse (pg. 37), which is not as distinctly tricolored and lacks the white-tipped tail (white tip on tail is not a reliable field mark). Jumping mice have longer tails than other mouse species. Often easy to differentiate by considering the habitat. The Meadow Jumping Mouse is seen in Michigan's open regions, while Woodland Jumping Mouse is often in coniferous forests in the northern part of the state.

Habitat: coniferous woodlands with much undergrowth, forest edges

Home: nest made of dried grass, under a clump of grass or fallen log; used for hibernation

Food: herbivore, insectivore; fungi, seeds, fruit, insects

Sounds: inconsequential; scratching or scampering can be heard, drums front feet on ground if threatened

Breeding: May-Jun mating; 23-29 days gestation; will mate shortly after emerging from hibernation

Young: 4-7 pups once per year; born naked with eyes closed, eyes open at 26 days, weaned at 1 month

(more information on next page) 41

Signs: surface runways leading in many directions, grasses with missing seed heads (topped), piles of grass stems that are the same length and have seed heads removed

Activity: nocturnal; active 5-6 months of the year, hibernating from October to April or May

Tracks: hind paw 1¼" (3 cm) long with a long narrow heel and 5 toes, forepaw ½" (1 cm) long with 4 toes; 1 set of 4 tracks; tracks seen only in mud during months of activity

Stan's Notes: One might conclude from its common name that this mouse jumps to get around. Actually, it usually walks on all four feet or moves in a series of small jumps. The common name comes from its ability to leap up to 4 feet (1.2 m) when startled or to escape predators. Jumps several times, then will often stay perfectly still to blend into the environment.

The only member of the genus *Napaeozapus*, this mouse rarely leaves the forest. A full one-third of its diet consists of fungi, with seeds and insects comprising the rest. Feeding on fungi provides the mouse with much needed water. The mouse deposits fungi spores through its excrement, which benefits the fungi.

Like the Meadow Jumping Mouse, Woodland Jumping Mouse is a hibernator, gaining up to 100 percent of its body weight in fat each fall. It is a true hibernator, not active until springtime, with most entering hibernation in October. Males emerge in April, females in May. Apparently many do not survive winter. Some studies indicate only half the population emerges the next spring.

Reproduces only once each year, while the Meadow Jumping Mouse reproduces twice. Its gestation period of up to about 4 weeks is much longer than the gestation of the Meadow Jumping Mouse, which is usually only 17-21 days. Gives birth to 4-7 young despite having only four teats, unlike Meadow Jumping Mouse, which has eight.

House Mouse
Mus musculus

Family: Rats and Mice (Muridae)

Size: L 2½-4" (6-10 cm); T 2-4" (5-10 cm)

Weight: ½-¾ oz. (14-21 g)

Description: Gray to light brown above, slightly lighter gray below. Large ears. Tail is gray above, naked and nearly the same length as the body.

Origin/Age: non-native; 1-2 years

Compare: Smaller than the White-footed Mouse (pg. 49) and Deer Mouse (pg. 53), but House Mouse has a naked tail and is grayer than other mice. One of the smaller mouse species in the state, making it easy to identify.

Habitat: houses, buildings, cultivated fields

Home: nest with a hollow center, mass of plant or man-made material such as paper or insulation

Food: herbivore, insectivore; seeds, vegetation, fruit, nuts, insects

Sounds: inconsequential; scampering or scratching can be heard

Breeding: Mar-Oct mating; 18-21 days gestation

Young: 2-15 pups 3-4 times per year; born naked with eyes closed

(more information on next page)

Signs: strong smell of urine in the areas it often visits; small, hard black droppings the size of a pinhead

Activity: nocturnal; active year-round

scat

Tracks: hind paw ½" (1 cm) long with 5 toes, forepaw ¼" (.6 cm) long with 4 toes; 1 set of 4 tracks; sometimes has a tail drag mark

Stan's Notes: One of the few non-native mammals in Michigan. Originally from central Asia. Aboard Spanish ships that landed in the New World in the sixteenth century, it was inadvertently introduced into North America.

Uncommon in undisturbed areas and frequently associated with people. Competes effectively with and often displaces native mice and voles, making it an unwanted species. Especially not wanted in homes since it is known to carry disease, damage structures and contaminate food. Must live in a heated dwelling such as a barn or home since it cannot tolerate cold or survive a northern winter. However, it thrives in fields in southern states without the assistance of protective structures.

White mice used in laboratory experiments are bred from albino mice of this species. The species name *musculus* comes from the Sanskrit word *musha*, meaning "thief," and refers to its habit of gathering or "stealing" large quantities of food from homes. Will chew just about anything. It even gnaws holes in wood, giving rise to the stereotypic mouse hole in the baseboard of a wall.

Lives in small to large groups and tolerates overpopulation well. Shares nests, burrows and tunnels with others of its species and performs mutual grooming. While other mouse species become carnivorous when there is overcrowding, a female House Mouse will simply reproduce less often or part of the group will migrate to a new location.

White-footed Mouse
Peromyscus leucopus

Family: Rats and Mice (Muridae)

Size: L 3-4¼" (7.5-10.5 cm); T 2-3½" (5-9 cm)

Weight: ⅜-1¼ oz. (11-35 g)

Description: Reddish brown back and sides with white chest, belly, legs and feet. Tail is brown above, white below and shorter than the head and body. Large bulging eyes. Large, round naked ears.

Origin/Age: native; 1-2 years

Compare: Hard to distinguish from Deer Mouse (pg. 53). White-footed Mouse is usually slightly smaller, with smaller ears and a slightly shorter tail. Deer Mouse is seen in nearly any habitat year-round. White-footed is primarily seen in woodlands and brushy habitats.

Habitat: woodlands, fields, around dwellings

Home: nest, loose round mass of plant material with a hollow center, lined with animal hair, milkweed silk or other soft material, usually underneath a log or other shelter or inside a log or standing tree; abandons nest when completely soiled with urine and builds another

Food: omnivore; seeds, vegetation, fruit, nuts, insects, baby birds, carrion

Sounds: inconsequential; scratching or scampering can be heard, drums front feet on ground if threatened

Breeding: Mar-Oct mating; 22-23 days gestation

Young: 4-6 pups up to 3 times per year; all gray when very young, dull brown after 40-50 days, reddish brown in a couple months

(more information on next page) 49

Signs: stockpiles of jewelweed seeds near nest, strong smell of urine in the areas it often visits; small, hard black scat the size of a pinhead

Activity: nocturnal in summer, more diurnal in winter; remains in the nest during the coldest winter days

Tracks: hind paw ¾" (2 cm) long with 5 toes, forepaw ¼" (.6 cm) long with 4 toes; 1 set of 4 tracks; sometimes has a tail drag mark

Stan's Notes: Not as common or widespread as the Deer Mouse, but more territorial and aggressive. Will bite when it is handled, unlike the more tame and mild-mannered Deer Mouse. Like the other mice, it is an important part of the ecosystem. It is prey for such animals as foxes, coyotes, hawks, owls and many more.

Its geographic range extends from the East coast to Montana and down through Arizona to southern Mexico. This mouse is a great swimmer that has dispersed to islands in the largest lakes.

An excellent climber, often climbing trees to find seeds. Uses its tail to help maintain balance when climbing. Enjoys a variety of foods, but consumes mainly seeds, favoring black cherry pits and jewelweed seeds. Will cache food in autumn close to its nest, often in a former bird nest. Enters homes in the fall in search of shelter and food.

pup

In the coldest winter months it enters a condition resembling hibernation (torpor), in which body temperature drops and rate of breathing slows from 700 breaths per minute to as few as 60.

Young are born with eyes and ears closed, but develop quickly. They leave their mothers after only 2 weeks and start to breed at about 40 days. Rarely lives more than one year, with entirely new populations produced annually. A carrier (vector) for ticks that carry Lyme disease.

Deer Mouse
Peromyscus maniculatus

Family: Rats and Mice (Muridae)

Size: L 3-4½" (7.5-11 cm); T 2-4" (5-10 cm)

Weight: ⅜-1¼ oz. (11-35 g)

Description: Back and sides highly variable in color from gray to reddish brown. Chest, belly, legs and feet are always white. Sharply bicolored tail, dark above and white below, as long as head and body. Large bulging eyes. Large round ears.

Origin/Age: native; 1-2 years

Compare: Tail is slightly longer than that of White-footed Mouse (pg. 49). However, it is extremely difficult to differentiate between these mice because of their remarkable similarities.

Habitat: nearly all habitats including woodlands, prairies, fields, wetlands and around dwellings

Home: nest made of dried plant material and moss, in a small depression in the ground or in an above-ground cavity

Food: omnivore; seeds, vegetation, fruit, nuts, insects, earthworms, baby birds, baby mice, carrion

Sounds: inconsequential; scratching or scampering can be heard, drums front feet on ground if threatened

Breeding: Mar-Oct mating; 21-25 days gestation

Young: 1-8 (average 5) pups up to 3 times per year; born naked and deaf with eyes closed, juvenile is gray with a white belly, leaves mother at 3 weeks

(more information on next page)

Signs: strong smell of urine in the areas it often visits, including its large nest made from dried plant material; small, hard black droppings the size of a pinhead

Activity: nocturnal, crepuscular; active year-round, stays in nest during the coldest winter days or during heavy rain in summer

Tracks: hind paw ¾" (2 cm) long with 5 toes, forepaw ¼" (.6 cm) long with 4 toes; 1 set of 4 tracks; sometimes has a tail drag mark, often a short single groove on the surface of snow between ridges of snow made by tunneling

Stan's Notes: The most common mouse in Michigan and the most widespread rodent in North America. Found in just about every habitat from the Arctic Circle to the rain forests in Central America. More than 100 subspecies have been described with several occurring in Michigan, including Prairie Deer Mouse and Woodland Deer Mouse; differences are in tail length and ear size. Deer Mice look different in different parts of the world (morphologically variable), more so than other mice species.

An important food source for other animals such as foxes, hawks, coyotes and owls. Lives mostly on the ground. Tunnels beneath snow to the surface of the ground and also runs around on top of snow. May have several emergency escape tunnels in addition to the tunnel that leads to its nest.

Very tame and not aggressive. Climbs trees and shrubs to reach seeds and leaves. Caches food for winter, storing seeds and small nuts in protected areas outside the nest.

Builds nest during late fall or early winter in a bluebird nest box or in another birdhouse if the box is not left open for the winter. Usually solitary, but will gather in small groups in winter, usually females with young, to huddle and conserve heat. However, their combined urine quickly soaks nesting material, necessitating a move to another nest box or natural cavity. Readily enters homes looking for shelter and food.

Sexually mature at 5-7 weeks. Male may stay with female briefly after mating, but frequently lives a solitary life. Female is more territorial than the male, but male has a larger home range. Home territory ranges from a few hundred square feet to a couple acres.

A primary host for the virulent hantavirus that causes Hantaviral Pulmonary Syndrome (HPS), a serious disease in humans. Great care must be taken not to breathe in dust or other debris when cleaning out a birdhouse with a Deer Mouse nest.

Norway Rat
Rattus norvegicus

Family: Rats and Mice (Muridae)

Size: L 8-10" (20-25 cm); T 5-8" (13-20 cm)

Weight: ½-1 lb. (.2-.5 kg)

Description: Brown to grayish brown above and gray below. Long narrow snout. Large round ears. Dark eyes. Scaly tail, shorter than the body length.

Origin/Age: non-native; 2-4 years

Compare: Larger than all species of mice, voles and shrews. Look for large ears, a long naked tail and narrow pointed snout to help identify. Smaller than the Muskrat (pg. 81), which is rarely seen away from water and never enters homes, barns and other buildings where Norway Rat is typically seen.

Habitat: almost always associated with people in places such as cities, dumps and farms

Home: network of interconnecting tunnels, 2-3 inches (5-7.5 cm) wide and up to 6 feet (1.8 m) long, leading to inner chambers used for sleeping and feeding, often has several escape exits and dead-end tunnels for hiding

Food: omnivore; seeds, nuts, insects, carrion, birds, bird eggs, small mammals

Sounds: high-pitched squeaks when squabbling with other rats; scratching or scampering can be heard

Breeding: year-round mating; 20-25 days gestation; female can mate within hours of giving birth

Young: 2-9 (average 6) offspring up to 10 times per year; born naked with eyes closed, eyes open at about 2 weeks, weaned at 3-4 weeks

(more information on next page) 57

Signs: holes chewed in barn walls or doors, well-worn paths along walls or that lead in and out of chewed holes, smell of urine near the nest site; large, hard, cylindrical, dark brown-to-black droppings, deposited along trails

scat

Activity: nocturnal; active year-round, can be active on cloudy days

Tracks: hind paw 1½" (4 cm) long with narrow heel and 5 toes, forepaw 1" (2.5 cm) long with 4 well-spread toes; often follows the same paths over and over, making individual tracks difficult to distinguish

Stan's Notes: A rat of cities large and small as well as rural areas, including farms. This animal has greatly benefited from its association with humans. It has adapted well to city environments, feeding on discarded food and carrion. In farm settings, it eats stored food such as grain.

Also known as Common Rat, Brown Rat, Water Rat or Sewer Rat. A good swimmer and climber. Tolerates cold temperatures well. Excavates by loosening dirt with its front feet, pushes dirt under its belly, then turns and pushes dirt out with its head and front feet. Will chew through roots when they are in the way. A true omnivore, it sometimes acts like a predator, killing chickens and other small farm animals. Able to reproduce quickly, especially when food is abundant.

Has a very small territory with a high population density. Will migrate upon occasion. Large numbers have been seen leaving an area, presumably in response to overcrowding and a dwindling food supply.

Despite its common name, the Norway Rat is thought to originate from central Asia. It was introduced to different parts of the world via trading ships in the 1600-1700s and is believed to have been brought to North America in ships that transported grain in the eighteenth century. The name "Norway" actually comes from the fact this species was scientifically described in Norway.

This is the same species as the white rats used in lab experiments. While it is not the species that carried the famed bubonic plague (Black Rat, *R. rattus*), it is still is a carrier of disease and fleas and should be exterminated whenever possible. However, it is hard to trap and exterminate since its home usually has several escape exits. Due to intense human pressure for eradication (artificial selection), it has become resistant to many types of rat poisons.

Southern Red-backed Vole
Clethrionomys gapperi

Family: Rats and Mice (Muridae)

Size: L 3-4" (7.5-10 cm); T 1-2" (2.5-5 cm)

Weight: 1-1½ oz. (28-43 g)

Description: A rusty red back with lighter brown sides. Black belly hair with white tips, making belly appear silvery white. Rounded snout. Small round ears. Small dark eyes. Short tail.

Origin/Age: native; 1-2 years

Compare: Smaller than Meadow Vole (pg. 69), which has a more grizzled appearance and is not as red. Also smaller than Prairie Vole (pg. 73), which is gray brown with no red. Voles have shorter, rounder snouts and shorter tails than mice.

Habitat: coniferous forests, spruce bogs, swamps, wetlands

Home: nest with a hollow center, made of plant material, 3-4 inches (7.5-10 cm) wide, underneath a log or among tree roots

Food: insectivore, herbivore; insects, green leaves, fruit, seeds, leaf buds, bark of young trees, fungi

Sounds: inconsequential; rarely, if ever, heard

Breeding: late winter to late autumn mating; 17-19 days gestation

Young: 2-8 (average 5) offspring several times per year; born naked and toothless with eyes closed, body covered with fine hair and eyes open by about 12 days, weaned and on its own at about 3 weeks, appears gray until 1-2 months, then turns red

(more information on next page)

Signs: runways in grass leading beneath rocks, cut grass piled up along runways

Activity: diurnal, nocturnal; active year-round, rests and sleeps for several hours, then is active for several hours throughout the day with peaks at dawn and dusk

Tracks: hind paw ¾" (2 cm) long with 5 toes, forepaw slightly smaller with 4 toes; individual tracks are indistinguishable and create a single groove

Stan's Notes: A very common vole. Coexists with Meadow Voles where their habitats overlap. This animal is a member of the Voles and Lemmings (Arvicolinae) subfamily, which is in the Rats and Mice (Muridae) family.

Even though this species is called Southern Red-backed Vole, it ranges from Michigan northward, all across southern Canada and coastal Alaska. The Northern Red-backed Vole (not shown) looks similar and is found in northern Canada and Alaska.

Southern Red-backed Vole is a food staple for many mammals such as foxes, Short-tailed Weasels and coyotes, and is also a major food item for many hawk and owl species.

A short-lived animal, with most living only 10-12 months; some, however, can survive as long as 24 months. Populations peak in autumn, with numbers dropping quickly during winter due to predation and starvation. Entire birds of prey populations may move when Southern Red-backed Vole populations drop.

Active day and night and does not hibernate. Carries on with life underneath snow (subnivean), even expanding its home range in that environment. Will follow well-maintained surface trails only occasionally, as does the Meadow Vole. May use tunnel systems of larger animals. Rarely enters homes or cabins. May store roots, shoots and fungi for later consumption. Underground fungi is an important and much sought-after food source.

Like all other voles species, the digestive tract of this species has a large pouch called a cecum, which contains microscopic bacteria (microflora). These microflora help to break down items that are hard to digest such as cellulose, which is the chief component of green plants.

Becomes sexually mature at 5-6 months. The male will stay with the family until the young are weaned.

Woodland Vole
Microtus pinetorum

Family: Rats and Mice (Muridae)

Size: L 3¾-4½" (9.5-11 cm); T ½-1¼" (1-3 cm)

Weight: ¾-1¼ oz. (21-35 g)

Description: Overall chestnut brown above with a gray chest and belly. Short round snout. Tiny eyes. Small, but visible ears. Short bicolored tail that changes gradually from dark on top to light below.

Origin/Age: native; 1-2 years

Compare: Smaller than Meadow Vole (pg. 69), which has a longer tail. The Prairie Vole (pg. 73) has a grizzled appearance, with longer, black-tipped fur. The Meadow and Prairie Voles have sharply bicolored tails unlike the gradually bicolored tail of the Woodland Vole.

Habitat: deciduous forests with thick leaf litter and green ground cover, dense grass patches

Home: ball-shaped nest with a hollow center, made of dried grasses, often belowground in a network of tunnels; lives mainly underground, also maintains a series of surface tunnels

Food: herbivore; green plants in summer; roots, fruits, bulbs and seeds in winter

Sounds: inconsequential; chatters with up to 5 notes per call when threatened

Breeding: Jan-Nov mating; 20-24 days gestation

Young: 1-4 pups up to 4 times per year; born with eyes and ears closed, weaned at 17 days

(more information on next page)

Signs: well-worn runways and tunnels through thick vegetation

Activity: nocturnal, diurnal; active year-round, often active 24 hours, with several hours of rest followed by several hours of activity

Tracks: hind paw ½-¾" (1-2 cm) long with 5 toes, forepaw ¼" (.6 cm) long with 4 toes; individual tracks are indistinguishable and create a single groove

Stan's Notes: A vole of deciduous forests that have a thick layer of decaying leaves and branches (duff). Sometimes called Pine Vole, which is somewhat of a misnomer since it does not spend much time in coniferous habitats. The Latin species name *pinetorum* is misleading since it refers to a pine habitat. Why these names have been applied is unknown. The genus name *Microtus* is Greek and refers to the small ears that are common to this genus.

The small body and ears, tiny eyes and large front claws suit it well for an underground (fossorial) life of digging. Digs out areas to cache food for consumption later.

The chestnut color, small size and unique tail help to identify the Woodland Vole. Its bicolored tail is unlike the tail of any other vole species, gradually changing from dark above to light below.

Can be semi-colonial, with several families sharing a single nest chamber. Doesn't seem to have the "peak and crash" population cycles common to other vole species.

Meadow Vole
Microtus pennsylvanicus

Family: Rats and Mice (Muridae)

Size: L 4-5" (10-13 cm); T 1½-2½" (4-6 cm)

Weight: 1-2½ oz. (28-71 g)

Description: Overall dark gray with rusty red highlights and peppered with black. Gray chest and belly. Short round snout. Ears small, but visible. Tail is dark above, light below.

Origin/Age: native; 1-2 years

Compare: Similar to the Prairie Vole (pg. 73), which has a shorter tail. Southern Red-backed Vole (pg. 61) has a redder coat and shorter tail. Woodland Vole (pg. 65) has a bicolored tail that changes from dark above to light below gradually, unlike the sharp demarcation of the Meadow Vole's tail.

Habitat: wet grassy meadows and fields, moist woodland edges

Home: ball-shaped nest with a hollow center, made of dried grass, often under a log or rock; lives above ground and belowground, maintains a system of trails and tunnels

Food: herbivore; green grass, seeds, sedges

Sounds: inconsequential; chatters, grinds teeth and drums hind feet on the ground when threatened

Breeding: Apr-Nov mating, sometimes will mate in winter; 21 days gestation

Young: 3-10 pups (average 7) up to 15 times per year; weaned at about 2 weeks

(more information on next page) 69

Signs: well-worn runways in the grass; piles of freshly cut grass stacked up along runways

Activity: diurnal, nocturnal; active year-round, often active 24 hours a day with several hours of rest followed by several hours of activity, less active on nights with a full moon

scat

Tracks: hind paw ¾" (2 cm) long with 5 toes, forepaw ½" (1 cm) long with 4 toes; individual tracks are indistinguishable and create a single groove

Stan's Notes: Sometimes mistakenly called Meadow Mouse or Field Mouse, but this is not a mouse and does not enter homes like mice. Fares well in abandoned farmlands and most places that are moist and have thick grass, including fields.

While many other small mammals include insects in their diet, this is one of the few small animals that is strictly vegetarian.

Thought to have a social system in which females are territorial, with males moving freely in and around female territories. Tends to be solitary during the breeding season and gathers in non-breeding groups in winter. During periods of activity, it maintains runways, feeds, finds a mate and marks territory with urine and feces.

pups

The most prolific mammal on earth by far, with the female able to reproduce at 3 weeks. Female has a postpartum estrus, which allows her to mate almost immediately after giving birth.

This species is preyed upon by many larger mammals and birds when the population is abundant. Population cycles swing up and down every 2-5 years; unknown why or how this happens.

Prairie Vole
Microtus ochrogaster

Family: Rats and Mice (Muridae)

Size: L 4-5" (10-13 cm); T 1-1½" (2.5-4 cm)

Weight: 1¼-2 oz. (35-57 g)

Description: Gray brown to yellow brown above, lighter gray below. Gray-tipped or black-tipped hair gives it a grizzled appearance. Short round snout. Short bicolored tail, dark above, lighter below. Ears are small and barely visible. Only 5 toe pads on the hind feet.

Origin/Age: native; 1-2 years

Compare: Larger than the more common Southern Red-backed Vole (pg. 61), which has a rusty red back, silvery white belly and longer tail. Southern Bog Lemming (pg. 77) has a shorter tail. Prairie Vole has 5 toe pads on its hind feet unlike other voles, which have 6.

Habitat: prairies, dry grassy meadows, dry fields

Home: ball-shaped nest with a hollow center, made from dried grass

Food: herbivore, insectivore; seeds, green grass, roots, tubers, insects

Sounds: inconsequential; rarely, if ever, heard

Breeding: May-Oct mating; 21 days gestation; most breed only a couple times each year

Young: 3-5 pups; born naked with pink skin, brown fur appears at about 2 days, crawls at about 5 days, eats solid food at about 12 days, leaves mother after only 2-3 weeks

(more information on next page) 73

runway

Signs: extensive system of aboveground, well-worn runways where grass is cut and removed, runways can be packed bare soil or lined with grass clippings; scat rarely seen

Activity: diurnal, nocturnal; active year-round, spends much of its time underground in dens, active in 4-hour cycles with more daytime activity in winter and less during hot summer months

Tracks: hind paw ¾-1" (2-2.5 cm) long with 5 toes, forepaw ½" (1 cm) long with 4 toes; individual tracks are indistinguishable and create a single groove

Stan's Notes: A vole of dry prairies. Since this is a rare habitat in Michigan, the Prairie Vole is less common than the Meadow Vole. Prairie Vole lives in dryer areas, while the Meadow Vole takes the wetter habitats where ranges overlap. Well adapted to life on the prairie, it creates burrows and maintains an extensive surface runway system. Will often cache extra seeds in its burrow system. Rarely a problem to people. A good food source for hawks, owls, foxes and other larger mammals.

Like other voles and the lemming, it has a large pouch (cecum) at the beginning of the colon. The cecum contains microscopic bacteria (microflora), which help break down cellulose, the main component in plant material.

Starts to breed at 4 weeks. A monogamous vole, with females producing small litters. Young apparently produce an ultrasonic sound that helps their parents find them in the dark.

Local populations can range from a few dozen to several hundred individuals per acre. During drought, females do not ovulate and reproduction drops. Reproduces throughout the year with peaks occurring from May through August. Specific peaks appear to be tied to the availability of moisture and increased production of grass, which shelters and feeds these animals. Populations peak every 2-4 years. These cycles are not well understood and are still being studied.

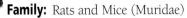

Southern Bog Lemming
Synaptomys cooperi

Family: Rats and Mice (Muridae)

Size: L 5-5½" (13-14 cm); T ½-1" (1-2.5 cm)

Weight: ¾-1¾ oz. (21-50 g)

Description: Uniquely shaped with head appearing larger than body. Reddish brown above, gray to silver below. Round ears are small, but visible. Extremely short tail, dark above, light below.

Origin/Age: native; 1-2 years

Compare: Larger than the Prairie Vole (pg. 73), which is gray with a grizzled appearance. Larger than the more common Red-backed Vole (pg. 61), which has a dark belly.

Habitat: grassy meadows, mixed and coniferous forests

Home: ball-shaped nest with inner chamber, sometimes up in a sphagnum mound (hummock) in a bog, usually underground in summer, almost always above ground during winter; constructs nest with shredded dried grass and leaves

Food: herbivore; grass, clover, other green plants

Sounds: inconsequential; rarely, if ever, heard

Breeding: May-Aug mating; 23-26 days gestation; female is able to mate 1 day after giving birth

Young: 2-6 offspring 2-3 times per year; born sparsely furred with eyes and ears closed, hears well at 7 days, eyes open at 12 days

(more information on next page)   77

Signs: neatly clipped piles of grass are often the only evidence of its presence, seen along well-maintained surface runways leading to and from nest; piles of green scat serve as signposts

Activity: diurnal, nocturnal; active year-round, moves about in a system of tunnels and aboveground runways, spends most of its time above ground, also active under snow in winter (subnivean)

Tracks: hind paw ¾" (2 cm) long with 5 toes, forepaw slightly smaller with 4 toes; individual tracks are indistinguishable and create a single track or groove

Stan's Notes: The Southern Bog Lemming has an unfortunate common name. It seldom inhabits bogs and is seen in grasslands and forested regions instead. Member of the Voles and Lemmings (Arvicolinae) subfamily, in the Rats and Mice (Muridae) family.

Few studies have been done nationally on bog lemmings, with even fewer done in Michigan, so not much is known about its natural history. It has a wide distribution in Michigan, but is not very common and not encountered frequently.

Moves around in a system of underground tunnels, most only about 6 inches (15 cm) below the surface of the ground. Uses a network of surface runways while gathering food, often caching leaves and other food along the runway system for consumption later. Also uses the tunnels and runways of other animals.

Muskrat
Ondatra zibethicus

Family: Rats and Mice (Muridae)

Size: L 8-12" (20-30 cm); T 7-12" (18-30 cm)

Weight: 1-4 lb. (.5-1.8 kg)

Description: Glossy dark brown, lighter on the sides and belly. Long naked tail, covered with scales and slightly vertically flattened (taller than it is wide). Small round ears. Tiny eyes.

Origin/Age: native; 3-10 years

Compare: Much smaller with a longer, thinner tail than the American Beaver (pg. 85), which has a large flat tail. Similar habitat as the Mink (pg. 173), which has a well-furred tail and a white patch on chin.

Habitat: ponds, lakes, ditches, small rivers

Home: small den, called a lodge, made of cattail leaves and other soft green (herbaceous) plant material, 1-2 underwater entrances, often has 1 chamber, sometimes a burrow in a lakeshore, larger dens may have 2 chambers with separate occupants

Food: herbivore, carnivore to a much lesser extent; aquatic plants, roots, cattail and bulrush shoots, roots and rhizomes; also eats dead fish, crayfish, clams, snails and baby birds

Sounds: inconsequential; chewing sounds can be heard when feeding above water on feeding platform

Breeding: Apr-Aug mating; 25-30 days gestation

Young: 6-7 offspring 2-3 times per year; born naked with eyes closed, swims at about 2 weeks, weaned at about 3 weeks

(more information on next page) 81

swimming

lodge

Signs: well-worn trails through vegetation along a lakeshore near a muskrat lodge, feeding platform made of floating plant material, 2 square feet (154.8 sq. cm), usually strewn with partially eaten cattails and other plants; lodge made of mud and cut vegetation, occasionally many lodges will dot the surface of a shallow lake

Activity: nocturnal, crepuscular; active all year, doesn't hibernate

Tracks: hind paw 2½-3½" (6-9 cm) long with 5 toes and a long heel, forepaw about half the size with 5 toes spread evenly; hind paws fall near or onto fore prints (direct register) when walking, often obliterating the forepaw tracks; prints may show only 4 toes since the fifth toe is not well formed, often has a tail drag mark

Stan's Notes: This animal is native only to North America, but it has been introduced all over the world. The musky odor (most evident in the male during breeding season) emanating from two glands near the base of the rat-like tail gives it the common name. Some say the common name is a derivation of the Algonquian Indian word *musquash*, which sounds somewhat like "muskrat."

Mostly aquatic, the muskrat is highly suited to living in water. It has a waterproof coat that protects it from frigid temperatures. Partially webbed hind feet and a fringe of hair along each toe help propel the animal. The tail, which is slightly flattened vertically, also helps with forward motion and is used as a rudder. Its mouth can close behind the front teeth only, allowing the animal to cut vegetation free while it is submerged.

A good swimmer that swims backward and sideways with ease. Able to stay submerged for up to 15 minutes. Surfaces to eat. May store some roots and tubers in mud below the water to consume during winter.

When small areas of a lake open up in winter, it will often sit on the ice to feed or sun itself. Although it lives in small groups, there is no social structure and individuals act mainly on their own. Becomes sexually mature the first spring after its birth.

Lodge building seems to concentrate in the fall. Not all muskrats build a mound-type lodge. Many dig a burrow in a lakeshore. A muskrat lodge is not like a beaver lodge, which is made with woody plant material. There is only one beaver lodge per lake or stream, while there are often several muskrat lodges in a body of water. Does not defecate in the lodge, so the interior living space of the lodge is kept remarkably clean.

Overcrowding can occur in fall and winter, causing individuals to travel great distances in spring to establish new homes. Many muskrats are killed when crossing roads during this season.

American Beaver
Castor canadensis

Family: Beavers (Castoridae)

Size: L 3-4' (1-1.2 m); T 7-14" (18-36 cm)

Weight: 20-60 lb. (9-27 kg)

Description: Reddish brown fur. Body often darker than head. Large, flat, naked black tail, covered with scales. Small round ears. Large, exposed orange incisors. Tiny eyes.

Origin/Age: native; 10-15 years

Compare: Much larger than Muskrat (pg. 81), which has a long narrow tail. Look for a large flat tail to help identify the American Beaver.

Habitat: rivers, streams, ponds, lakes, ditches

Home: den, called a lodge, hollow inside with holes on top for ventilation, 1-2 underwater entrances; beavers that live on rivers often dig burrows in riverbanks rather than constructing dens

Food: herbivore; soft bark, inner bark, aquatic plants, green leaves

Sounds: loud slap created by hitting the surface of water with tail before diving when alarmed, chewing or gnawing sounds when feeding or felling trees

Breeding: Jan-Mar mating; 120 days gestation

Young: 1-8 kits once per year; about 1 lb. (.5 kg); born well furred with eyes open, able to swim within 1 week

(more information on next page)

tail slap

lodge

scat

Signs: dam and lodge made from large woody branches can indicate current or former activity since structures remain well after the beaver has moved on or been killed, chewed tree trunks with large amounts of wood chips at the base of trees, flattened paths through vegetation leading to and from a lake; oval pellets, 1" (2.5 cm) long, containing sawdust-like material and bark, scat seldom on land

Activity: nocturnal, crepuscular; active year-round, even under ice and when in lodge during winter

Tracks: hind paw 5" (13 cm) long with 5 toes pointing forward and long narrow heel, forepaw 3" (7.5 cm) with 5 splayed toes; wide tail drag mark often wipes out paw prints

Stan's Notes: Largest member of the Rodentia order in Michigan. Body is well suited for swimming. Valves close off the ears and nostrils when underwater, and a clear membrane covers the eyes. Can remain submerged up to 15 minutes. Webbed toes on hind feet help it swim as fast as 6 miles (10 km) per hour. Special lips seal the mouth yet leave the front incisors exposed, allowing it to carry branches in its mouth without water getting inside. At the lodge, it eats the soft bark of smaller branches the way we eat corn on the cob. Doesn't eat the interior wood. Stores branches for winter use by sticking them in mud on a lake or river bottom.

Has a specialized claw on each hind foot that is split like a comb and is used for grooming. Secretes a pungent oily substance (castor) from glands near the base of its tail. Castor is used to mark territories or boundaries called castor mounds.

Monogamous and mates for life. However, will take a new mate if partner is lost. Can live up to 20 years in captivity.

Young remain with parents through their first winter. They help cut and store a winter food source and maintain the dam while parents raise another set of young. Young disperse at two years.

Builds a dam to back up a large volume of water, creating a pond. Cuts trees at night by gnawing trunks. Uses larger branches to construct the dam and lodge. Cuts smaller branches and twigs of felled trees into 6-foot (1.8 m) sections. Dam repair is triggered by the sound of moving water, not by sight. Most repair activity takes place at night.

No other mammal besides humans changes its environment as much as beavers. Beaver ponds play an important role in moose populations. Moose feed on aquatic plants, cool themselves and escape biting insects in summer in beaver ponds. Other animals such as frogs, turtles and many bird species including ducks, herons and egrets also benefit from the newly created habitat.

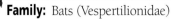

Little Brown Bat
Myotis lucifugus

Family: Bats (Vespertilionidae)

Size: L 1½-2" (4-5 cm); T 1¼-1¾" (3-4.5 cm); W 8-10" (20-25 cm)

Weight: ⅒-½ oz. (3-14 g)

Description: Overall brown. Dark, membranous naked wings and tail. Lighter brown-to-tan belly. Dark, pointed naked ears with a short round tragus. Small bright black eyes. Female slightly larger than male.

Origin/Age: native; 15-20 years

Compare: Nearly identical to the Big Brown Bat (pg. 105), which is larger and tends to roost in houses in winter. Little Brown Bat winter roosts in caves.

Habitat: forests, urban and suburban areas, farmlands

Home: female colonies in home attics, church steeples, barns and other buildings and solitary males in buildings and trees during summer, all in caves and mines during winter

Food: insectivore; small flying insects such as caddis flies, mayflies, midges and mosquitoes

Sounds: rapid series of high-pitched clicking noises, high-pitched squeaks of pups calling persistently to mother after she leaves to feed

Breeding: Aug-Sep mating before hibernation; 60-62 days gestation; sperm stored in the reproductive tract until the spring following mating

Young: 1 pup once per year from May to July; about one-fourth the weight of mother, born breach and naked with eyes closed, feeds on mother's milk only for first 18-20 days, flies at 18-25 days

(more information on next page)

Signs: piles of dark brown-to-black scat under roosting sites

Activity: nocturnal; active only on warm dry nights, comes out 20-30 minutes after sunset, returns to roost before sunrise

Tracks: none

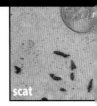

scat

Stan's Notes: One of the smallest and most common bats in the state. Many people construct large wooden bat houses to provide daytime roosts for this species. The genus name *Myotis* means "mouse ear" in Latin and presumably was given for its small mouse-like ears.

Often forages for food over rivers and lakes, beneath streetlights and wherever large groups of flying insects congregate. Locates prey by emitting a high-frequency (40-80 kHz) sound (which is inaudible to humans) and listens for returning echoes (echolocation). These calls are emitted approximately 20 times per second and increase to 200 times per second when honing in on prey.

This bat typically eats about half its body weight in insects every night. A lactating female can eat up to 110 percent of her weight in food nightly. The high volume of insect consumption makes this tiny animal desirable to have around. Farmers benefit greatly from its voracious appetite.

Females gather in maternity colonies of up to 75 individuals, sometimes more. A mother does not carry her pup when she is feeding or hunting, but will do so when threatened. Positioned across her chest, a pup holds one of her nipples with its mouth while its feet hold onto the opposite side of her body underneath her wing.

Spends winters in caves and mines. Flies up to several hundred miles to return to the same cave each year due to a strong attachment to its winter roost. Bats need to build up enough fat in the body to sustain them for the entire winter, which can last more than six months. If disturbed during hibernation, the body often uses up too much fat and does not leave enough in reserve to last until spring. Many bats, usually the young ones, die as a result. Thus, these caves and mines should never be disturbed.

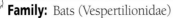

Eastern Pipistrelle
Pipistrellus subflavus

Family: Bats (Vespertilionidae)

Size: L 2-2¼" (5-5.5 cm); T 1-1¾" (2.5-4.5 cm); W 8-10" (20-25 cm)

Weight: ⅒-⅕ oz. (3-6 g)

Description: A tiny bat. Back is overall reddish to light brown. Chest and belly are paler. Individual hairs on the back are tricolored with a dark base, pale middle and dark tip. Membranous wings, dark brown to nearly black. Round dark ears with a thin blunt tragus. Tiny dark eyes.

Origin/Age: native; 10-15 years

Compare: Larger than Little Brown Bat (pg. 89), which is darker brown.

Habitat: wide variety such as deciduous forests, suburban and urban areas, farmlands

Home: medium to large maternity groups and alone in hollow trees, behind loose bark and in buildings during the summer, hundreds (sometimes up to thousands) in caves and mines during winter

Food: insectivore; small flying insects such as moths, crane flies, other flies and midges

Sounds: rapid series of high-pitched clicking noises

Breeding: Aug-Sep mating before hibernation; 60-65 days gestation; sperm stored in the reproductive tract until the spring following mating

Young: 1-2 (usually 2) pups once per year from June to early July; about one-fifth the weight of mother, born naked with eyes closed; flies at 14-22 days

(more information on next page)

Signs: flying bats in a slow fluttering pattern with an uneven direction like a moth, frequently in small groups; piles of dark brown-to-black scat under roosting sites

Activity: nocturnal; active only on warm dry nights, comes out at sunset, returns to roost before sunrise

Tracks: none

Stan's Notes: A semi-social cave bat, the tiny Eastern Pipistrelle is one of the most common and widely distributed bat species in eastern U.S. forests.

One of the first bat species to come out after sunset each night. Has a slow, fluttering flight pattern with an uneven direction, much like a flying moth. This slower, uneven flight seems to help the bat find more food since it is able to cover more air space. Will hunt above the tree line over ponds and streams for small flying insects such as moths. To locate prey, gives an ultrasonic emission that is impossible to hear (inaudible) by humans.

Spends the summer adding enough body fat to last the entire winter while it hibernates in a cave or a mine. However, little is known about its summer feeding and roosting behaviors.

This is the least cold-tolerant bat and the first bat species to enter caves and mines to hibernate, in late September to early October. Will migrate a short distance to the cave each year, often less than 50 miles (81 km). Strongly attached to the wintering cave and even to the exact spot within a cave. Generation after generation of bats return to the same cave every year. Seems to prefer large caves that face east, with stable temperatures near 50°F (10°C). Often roosts deeper in caves and mines than other bat species. Frequently covered with tiny water droplets during hibernation, which give it a whitish appearance. Since it does not emerge until April or May, it spends more time hibernating than it does being active during warm weather.

Females often form medium-sized maternity colonies of up to 50 individuals in spring. One of the few species of bats that routinely gives birth to twins.

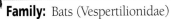

Northern Myotis
Myotis septentrionalis

Family: Bats (Vespertilionidae)

Size: L 2-2½" (5-6 cm); T 1½-1¾" (4-4.5 cm); W 8-10" (20-25 cm)

Weight: ⅕-⅜ oz. (6-11 g)

Description: Back is dull brown to yellow brown. Pale, nearly yellow belly. Membranous wings, dark brown to nearly black. Large, round dark ears with a long, thin pointed tragus. Tiny dark eyes.

Origin/Age: native; 10-15 years

Compare: Larger and more of a forest dweller than the Little Brown Bat (pg. 89), which is darker brown, has shorter ears and a less pronounced tragus. Look for a long, thin pointed tragus to help identify the Northern Myotis.

Habitat: wide variety such as deciduous forests, suburban and urban areas, farmlands

Home: behind loose bark, shingles, boards, shutters and beneath bridges and in concrete culverts during summer, caves and mines during winter

Food: insectivore; small flying insects such as moths, crane flies, other flies and midges

Sounds: rapid series of high-pitched clicking noises

Breeding: Sep-Oct mating before hibernation; 50-60 days gestation; sperm stored in the reproductive tract until the spring following mating

Young: 1 pup once per year from June to early July; about one-fourth the weight of the mother, born naked with eyes closed, flies at 30-37 days

(more information on next page) 97

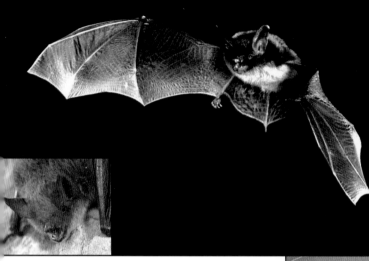

Signs: flying bats chasing moths after dark

Activity: nocturnal; active only on warm dry nights, comes out approximately 20 minutes after sunset, returns to roost before sunrise

scat

Tracks: none

Stan's Notes: The only range of the Northern Myotis is east of the Rockies, extending into eastern Canada. Where it does occur, it is not very common. Until 1979, it was considered a subspecies of Keen's Myotis (*M. keenii*), which is found only in the Pacific Northwest. Also called Northern Long-eared Myotis.

This solitary cave bat collects insects from the surface of leaves or the ground. Often finds moths and other insect prey by honing in on the sound produced by fluttering wings. Uses echolocation by emitting short pulses, 1-2 milliseconds long, at 40-120 kHz. These very low-intensity pulses don't travel very far. As measured by most bat detectors, the emissions only travel a distance of up to 6 feet (1.8 m) compared with up to 30 feet (9.1 m) for many other bats. Often carries its prey back to a perch to eat, enabling it to feed on larger insects than those eaten by other bats.

Females will frequently form small maternity colonies of up to 30 individuals in spring. Colonies usually are found behind a large piece of loose tree bark. Like other females of the genus *Myotis*, the female Northern Myotis bears a single pup each year that weighs about a fourth of her own weight. This would compare to a human female weighing 150 pounds (68 kg) giving birth to a 38-pound (17.1 kg) baby.

Makes a short annual migration to a cave for the winter. Will also hibernate in a mine. Can be seen in large groups in fall near cave entrances. Will hang from cave walls, but most squeeze into rock crevices. Some males never leave the area around their winter caves. Caves are well established and are used for centuries. These places need to be protected from disturbances during the winter, when bats are most vulnerable.

Evening Bat
Nycticeius humeralis

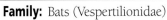

Family: Bats (Vespertilionidae)

Size: L 1¾-2¾" (4.5-7 cm); T 1¼-1½" (3-4 cm); W 13-14" (33-36 cm)

Weight: ⅛-¼ oz. (4-7 g)

Description: Overall reddish brown with a lighter brown belly. Blackish face, wings and feet. Large oval ears with a short curved tragus.

Origin/Age: native; 15-20 years

Compare: Smaller than the Big Brown Bat (pg. 105), which has a short round tragus.

Habitat: deciduous forests, near open fields and ponds

Home: maternity colonies in old buildings and hollow trees in summer, solitary males in old buildings and hollow trees year-round; presumably only females migrate to southern climates in winter

Food: insectivore; small flying insects such as moths, beetles, leafhoppers and flies

Sounds: rapid series of high-pitched clicking noises

Breeding: Oct-Nov mating in southern locations; unknown days gestation; sperm is stored in reproductive tract until the spring following mating

Young: 1-3 (usually 2) pups once per year in June; flies at 28-30 days

(more information on next page) 101

Signs: piles of dark brown-to-black scat at the base of large trees (made by roosting maternity colonies) and inside barns and other buildings

Activity: nocturnal; active just after sunset over open fields, ponds and farmlands, returns to roost before sunrise

Tracks: none

Stan's Notes: A widespread bat of southern states from Florida to Texas and north to Illinois and Pennsylvania, with its northern range barely reaching southern parts of Michigan. Populations are decreasing in part of its northern range, likely due to the removal of large dead trees and old structures such as barns.

Like other bats, the Evening Bat is a unique mammal because its forearms are specialized for true flight. Membranous skin that is an extension of the skin of the back and belly connects the body with the wings, legs and tail. Unlike birds, bats utilize both their wings and legs during flight.

Presumably, females in the northern part of the range migrate to southern climates during winter, where they meet with males to mate. Only females return north in spring, leaving the solitary males behind.

Almost never hibernates in caves or mines. Apparently remains active all winter in warm overwintering sites.

Maternity colony size ranges from 30-300 individuals. The ratio of females to males at birth is about equal, but nursing mothers give preference to female pups to the exclusion of males, causing a high mortality rate in young males.

Big Brown Bat
Eptesicus fuscus

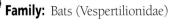

Family:	Bats (Vespertilionidae)
Size:	L 2-3" (5-7.5 cm); T 1½-2" (4-5 cm); W 13-14" (33-36 cm)
Weight:	½-⁹⁄₁₀ oz. (14-26 g)
Description:	Overall brown. Dark, membranous naked wings and tail. Lighter brown belly. Dark, oval naked ears with a short round tragus. Bright black eyes. Pointed snout.
Origin/Age:	native; 15-20 years
Compare:	Nearly identical but larger than Little Brown Bat (pg. 89), which winter roosts in caves. Big Brown Bat tends to winter roost in houses.
Habitat:	wide variety such as deciduous forests, suburban and urban areas, farmlands
Home:	walls and attics of homes, churches, barns and other buildings year-round, maternity colonies also in hollow trees
Food:	insectivore; small to large flying insects such as mosquitoes and beetles
Sounds:	rapid series of high-pitched clicking noises, high-pitched squeaks of pups calling persistently to mother after she leaves to feed can be heard from a distance of up to 30 feet (9.1 m) away
Breeding:	Aug-Sep mating before hibernation; 60-62 days gestation; sperm stored in the reproductive tract until the spring following mating
Young:	1-2 (usually 2) pups once per year from May to July; one-third the weight of mother, born breach and naked with eyes closed, flies at 18-35 days

(more information on next page) 105

Signs: piles of dark brown-to-black scat under roosting sites

Activity: nocturnal; active only on warm dry nights, comes out approximately 30 minutes after sunset, feeds until full, roosts the rest of night, returns to daytime roost before sunrise

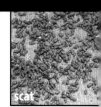
scat

Tracks: none

Stan's Notes: A common bat in Michigan. Found across North America from Maine to Washington and south to Central America and Florida. This is a fast-flying bat, reaching speeds of up to 25 miles (40 km) per hour.

Studies show that this species feeds on many crop and forest pests and insects, making it one of America's most beneficial animals and very desirable to have around. Has an erratic flight pattern as it swoops and dives for flying insects. Will often forage over rivers and lakes, underneath streetlights or anywhere large groups of flying insects congregate. Emits a high-frequency (27-48 kHz) sound (inaudible to humans) to locate prey and listens for returning echoes (echolocation). Most of these bats catch and eat one insect every three seconds, consuming $\frac{1}{10}$ ounce (3 g) per hour. During summer when rapidly growing pups demand increasing amounts of milk, a lactating female can consume up to $\frac{7}{10}$ ounce (20 g) of insects every night, which is nearly equal to her own body weight.

Will rarely winter in caves, preferring to roost alone or in small groups. Males are generally solitary in spring and summer.

Females will gather in maternity colonies of up to 75 individuals. Loyal to these maternal roosts, females return to them year after year. Approximately 80 percent of females give birth to two pups at the maternal roosts in spring and early summer.

A mother does not carry her pups during flight, but leaves them clinging to the roost until she returns. Holds pups to her chest under a wing to nurse. Recognizes young by their vocalizations.

Homeowners frequently discover these bats when remodeling or adding onto their homes during winter months. Any unwanted bat found in homes should be professionally moved or removed to avoid hurting the animal.

male

Red Bat
Lasiurus borealis

Family: Bats (Vespertilionidae)

Size: L 2-3" (5-7.5 cm); T 1¾-2¼" (4.5-5.5 cm); W 13-14" (33-36 cm)

Weight: ¼-½ oz. (7-14 g)

Description: Fur of male is red to orange, while female is dull red to chestnut (fur of both is sometimes frosted white). Membranous naked wings and tail, reddish brown to dark pink. White chest and belly. Round ears with a small triangular tragus. Bright black eyes. Tail extends directly behind the body.

Origin/Age: native; 15-20 years

Compare: Slightly larger than the Little Brown Bat (pg. 89) and similar size as the Big Brown Bat (pg. 105), both of which are brown, not red to orange.

Habitat: wide variety such as deciduous forests, edges of woods, urban and suburban areas, farmlands

Home: trees and shrubs during summer; migrates out of state in fall

Food: insectivore; flying insects such as moths, beetles, flies and leafhoppers, terrestrial insects such as grasshoppers and crickets

Sounds: rapid series of high-pitched clicking noises

Breeding: Aug-Sep mating during fall migration; 80-90 days gestation; sperm is stored in the reproductive tract until the spring following mating

Young: 1-5 (average 3) pups once per year from June to early July; born naked and helpless with eyes closed, flies at 30-42 days

(more information on next page)

male

female

Signs: extremely fast-flying bats close to forests after dark, one of the earlier fliers in the evening

Activity: nocturnal; active only on warm dry nights, comes out 10-20 minutes after sunset, returns to tree roost before sunrise

Tracks: none

Stan's Notes: This is the most abundant tree bat species in North America. Found wherever trees are present from east of the Rocky Mountains to the East coast and from Canada to Florida. Also called Eastern Red Bat.

One of the few mammals that has a color difference between the male and female. Its long dense fur keeps it warm during cold weather. Known to survive temperatures as low as 23°F (-5°C). Makes an ultrasonic call that cannot be heard by humans.

A very fast-flying bat, reaching speeds up to 40 miles (64 km) per hour. Flies back and forth along forest edges, across clearings in woods and underneath streetlights, hunting for moths and other insects. Often uses the same flight paths at night when searching for food.

Hangs alone in trees, usually along forest edges, in open fields or along streams. Appears to prefer roosting on the south side of a tree, where it is protected and shaded by leaves during the day. Usually doesn't return to the same daytime roost. Will hang from one foot, curl its head in toward its furry chest and wrap itself up in its membranous wings and tail. Often twists and turns in the wind while roosting, appearing like a dead leaf. Remains within a small home range of up to 2 acres (1 ha).

Migrates to southeastern and southwestern states, often in large flocks. Males and females appear to migrate at different times and to different summering grounds. However, they share wintering areas, where they apparently hibernate. Will emerge on warm nights to feed during winter.

Unlike the other bat species, pregnant females roost and mothers rear their young singly. One of the few bat species that produces more than one or two offspring per year. The only bat species with four nipples.

Silver-haired Bat

Lasionycteris noctivagans

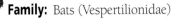

Family: Bats (Vespertilionidae)

Size: L 2-3" (5-7.5 cm); T 1½-1¾" (4-4.5 cm); W 13-14" (33-36 cm)

Weight: ¼-½ oz. (7-14 g)

Description: Overall dark brown to nearly black. Heavy frost of white or silver on back and neck. Membranous wings, dark brown to nearly black. Small, round dark ears with a small triangular tragus. Bright black eyes.

Origin/Age: native; 10-15 years

Compare: Smaller than Hoary Bat (pg. 121), which is tan with an overall silvery white appearance, creamy yellow throat and reddish brown wings and tail.

Habitat: wide variety such as deciduous forests, suburban and urban areas, farmlands

Home: alone or in small maternity colonies in trees or shrubs, behind loose bark, in hollow trunks or branches, sometimes in houses and barns during summer; migrates out of state in fall

Food: insectivore; flying insects such as moths, beetles, crane flies, other flies, leafhoppers and midges

Sounds: rapid series of high-pitched clicking noises

Breeding: Sep-Oct mating during fall migration; 50-60 days gestation; sperm stored in the reproductive tract until the spring following mating

Young: 1-2 (usually 2) pups once per year from June to early July; born naked and helpless with eyes closed, flies at 30-37 days

(more information on next page) 113

Signs: slow-flying bats around treetop level close to forests after dark, one of the earliest fliers in the evening, some appearing while it is still light

Activity: nocturnal; active only on warm dry nights, comes out at sunset, returns to the tree roost before sunrise

Tracks: none

Stan's Notes: One of the most easily recognizable bat species due to its heavily frosted dark fur. The genus and species names come from Greek and Latin words and translate into "night wandering shaggy bat."

One of the first bat species to be recognized as migratory. However, male and female bats spend their summers apart. Females are seen in the Midwest and East, while males are seen in western North America. Both sexes spend winters in southeastern and southwestern states. Therefore, any Silver-haired Bat found in Michigan is presumed to be a female or juvenile. While it is believed that this bat migrates out of Michigan, there is some evidence that at least a few will stay and hibernate in caves. During spring, females will often form small maternity colonies.

A relatively slow flyer that catches mostly slow-flying, soft-bodied insects such as moths. Like the other bat species, it drinks when flying, dipping its open mouth into water while skimming over the surface. Gives an ultrasonic call that humans can't hear. Able to lower its body temperature, heart rate and respiration to save energy during hibernation.

Associated more with old-growth forests than any other bat. It is estimated that this species requires at least 40 standing dead trees per acre to provide enough good roosting spots.

Indiana Bat
Myotis sodalis

Family: Bats (Vespertilionidae)

Size: L 1¾-3½" (4.5-9 cm); T 1-1¾" (2.5-4.5 cm); W 8-10" (20-25 cm)

Weight: ⅛-¼ oz. (4-7 g)

Description: Overall dark brown with pink highlights. Naked skin on face appears pink. Oval ears with a short round tragus. Tiny feet with short hairs on toes.

Origin/Age: native; 15-20 years

Compare: Larger than the Little Brown Bat (pg. 89). Look for pink highlights on fur to help identify.

Habitat: deciduous forests, near streams and creeks

Home: maternity colonies under loose bark and solitary males in trees in summer, all in caves and mines in winter in large, tightly packed colonies

Food: insectivore; small flying insects such as moths

Sounds: rapid series of high-pitched clicking noises, pups make high-pitched squeaks when their mother returns after feeding

Breeding: Sep-Oct mating before hibernation; unknown days gestation; sperm is stored in reproductive tract until the spring following mating

Young: 1 pup once per year from May to June; flies at 28-30 days

(more information on next page) 117

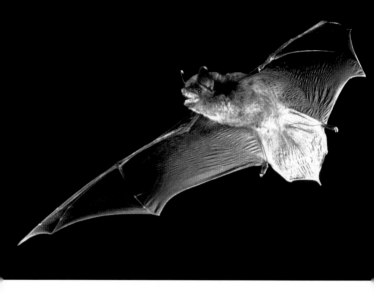

Signs: piles of dark brown-to-black scat at the base of large trees (made by roosting maternity colonies)

Activity: nocturnal; active only on warm dry nights, comes out at sunset, returns to roost before sunrise

Tracks: none

Stan's Notes: Federal and state endangered species. A systematic search for this bat, however, hasn't been conducted in Michigan.

Normally ranges from Indiana, Ohio, Missouri and Kentucky to as far east and north as Vermont. It has a short migration each fall to caves and mines in the southern part of the range.

Most arrive at winter cave or mine sites a few weeks ahead of time to breed before hibernation. Will swarm at the mouth of a cave or mine or just inside the cavity. Mates at night, sometimes on the ceiling at entrances to large caves.

Groups hibernate inside caves and mines that have the right temperature and humidity. Hibernating Indiana Bats can have a density of up to 300 or more bats per square foot. This high density makes them vulnerable to disturbances such as people entering the sites.

Migrates in spring to traditional sites where up to 100 females gather in maternity colonies to give birth and raise young. The colonies are usually under the bark of Shagbark Hickory or other trees. Females normally give birth to only one pup during spring, making their reproductive rates low. Overall populations are declining, with an estimated 300,000 Indiana Bats remaining.

Hoary Bat
Lasiurus cinereus

Family: Bats (Vespertilionidae)

Size: L 2-4" (5-10 cm); T 1¾-2½" (4.5-6 cm); W 15-16" (38-40 cm)

Weight: ¾-1¼ oz. (21-35 g)

Description: Tan fur with frosted tips, giving an overall silvery white (hoary) appearance. Creamy yellow throat. Membranous semi-naked wings and tail, reddish brown to dark brown. Round ears with a dark naked edge and short curved tragus. Large, bright black eyes. Female slightly larger than male.

Origin/Age: native; 15-20 years

Compare: Larger than Silver-haired Bat (pg. 113), which also has silvery frosted appearance but has black fur rather than tan. Easy to identify by its large size and hoary fur.

Habitat: wide variety such as deciduous and coniferous forests, urban and suburban areas, farmlands

Home: trees during summer; migrates out of state in fall

Food: insectivore; large flying insects such as, moths, beetles, flies, dragonflies, wasps and bees

Sounds: rapid series of high-pitched clicking noises

Breeding: Sep-Oct mating during fall migration; 60-62 days gestation; sperm stored in the reproductive tract until the spring following mating

Young: 1-4 (average 2) pups once per year from mid-May to early July; born helpless with fine silver hair on the body except for belly and with eyes closed, eyes open at 12 days, feeds on mother's milk only for up to 30 days, flies at 30-33 days

(more information on next page)

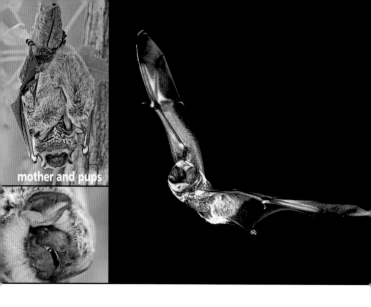

mother and pups

Signs: strong direct flight, appears like a bird

Activity: nocturnal; active only on warm dry nights, comes out approximately 1 hour or later after sunset, returns to tree roost before sunrise

Tracks: none

Stan's Notes: This is the largest and most widespread bat species in North America. Found throughout most of Canada, the U.S. and in parts of Central and South America. It is Hawaii's only native land mammal. Sometimes associated with the Red Bat.

A migratory species, with females populating the northern and eastern portions of the U.S., and males staying in the Southwest year-round. Mates during autumn migration, when females meet with males in southwestern states. After mating, females continue to migrate and winter in tropical regions of Central and South America. Females frequently will migrate with some bird species. The strong, direct flight pattern helps this bat keep up with birds, which are more agile. Some may not migrate and are thought to hibernate, but not much is known about this behavior. Females return to Michigan in the spring.

Not attracted to bat houses or human dwellings, this bat remains hidden in tree foliage during the day. Typically roosts 10-15 feet (3-4.5 m) high in trees. Comes out well after dark and usually makes one long foraging flight, up to 25 miles (40 km), before returning to its home range to spend the rest of the night.

Apparently likes to eat moths more than do other species of bats. Like other bats, it locates its prey by emitting a high-frequency sound that is inaudible to humans and listening for the returning echoes (echolocation).

The female is solitary. Unlike the other bats, the female Hoary Bat does not need to build up a large fat reserve for hibernation since it migrates to warmer climates that have adequate food supplies. Gives birth to pups while hanging from a tree branch that is often concealed by leaves. Mother does not carry her young when she feeds. Pups hang from a twig or leaf while the mother forages for food at night, but they cling to her during the day.

Least Chipmunk
Tamias minimus

Family: Squirrels (Sciuridae)

Size: L 4-5" (10-13 cm); T 3-4" (7.5-10 cm)

Weight: 2-3 oz. (57-85 g)

Description: Overall brown fur with alternating dark and light stripes from nose to base of tail. Orange brown sides with a lighter brown rump. Chin, chest and belly are pale white to gray. Long orange brown tail, nearly the length of the body, usually with a thin dark line running the entire length.

Origin/Age: native; 2-4 years

Compare: Smaller than its more common cousin, Eastern Chipmunk (pg. 129), which has a reddish brown rump, stripes on body that stop before the base of tail and less pronounced stripes on face.

Habitat: rocky outcrops, cliffs, roadsides, dry and open coniferous forests

Home: burrow, entrance usually a small round hole with no trace of excavated dirt, sometimes at the base of a rock, occasionally nests in a tree, may have different burrows in summer and winter, winter burrows are deeper underground

Food: omnivore; seeds, fruit, nuts, insects, fungi, buds, flowers, frogs, baby birds, bird eggs, small snakes

Sounds: distinctive high-pitched series of "chip" notes that sound a small bird, similar to Eastern Chipmunk

Breeding: Mar-Apr mating; 28-30 days gestation

Young: up to 7 offspring 1-2 times per year; born naked with eyes closed, weaned at about 60 days

(more information on next page) 125

Signs: piles of cracked seeds and acorns and other food on a log or large rock; oblong dark brown pellets, ⅛" (.3 cm) long, often not seen and not key in identifying this species

Activity: diurnal; does not come out on cold rainy days

Tracks: hind paw ¾-1¼" (2-3 cm) long with 5 toes, forepaw with 4 toes is about half the size of hind paw; 1 set of 4 tracks; hind paws fall in front of fore prints; tracks rarely seen since it lives in a dry rocky habitat and usually does not come out from burrow when snow is on the ground

Stan's Notes: This is the smallest and most widespread of the 22 chipmunk species in North America. Ranges from Michigan's Upper Peninsula north and west across Canada to the Yukon and south to the Rocky Mountains. With the exception of Least and Eastern Chipmunks, all others are found in western states. Home range is estimated at ¼ acre (.1 ha), with overlapping boundaries.

Like the other chipmunks, this one has fur-lined internal cheek pouches for carrying food and other items such as dirt while it excavates tunnels. Often runs with tail held vertically. When on a sun-dappled forest floor or in a rocky habitat, its bold stripes provide a great camouflage.

Comfortable climbing trees to gather seeds, buds and flowers for food. Stores large amounts of seeds, nuts and dried berries in an underground cavity. Feeds on its cache when it can't get outside due to weather. Known to steal food from neighboring "chippie" caches. One study has reported that nearly 500 acorns and 1,000 cherry pits were found in a Least Chipmunk cache.

Can become tame and even very bold, seeking people for hand-outs in areas with increased human contact. Often lives in close association with Eastern Chipmunks with no apparent conflict.

Enters its winter burrow later than the Eastern Chipmunk. Does not add a thick layer of fat in preparation for winter. Instead, it will cache food and sleep for 1-2 weeks at a time, waking to feed. Drifts into a state of deep sleep called torpor, which includes a mild metabolic rate drop, but not to the level of true hibernation.

Matures sexually at 10-12 months. Breeding season begins in late March or early April and lasts only a few weeks. Female can have up to two litters per season, but this is not common.

Eastern Chipmunk
Tamias striatus

Family: Squirrels (Sciuridae)

Size: L 6-8" (15-20 cm); T 3-4" (7.5-10 cm)

Weight: 3-5 oz. (85-142 g)

Description: Overall reddish brown with a single white stripe bordered by 2 dark stripes on each side running from nose to rump. Stripes are less prominent on face. Chin, chest and belly are pale white to gray. Reddish brown rump. Reddish brown tail, half the length of body.

Origin/Age: native; 2-4 years

Compare: Larger than Least Chipmunk (pg. 125), which is less common and has more pronounced stripes on the face.

Habitat: deciduous and coniferous forests, forest edges, near stone walls, rock piles or human dwellings

Home: burrow with several round entrance holes, each 2 inches (5 cm) wide with no trace of excavated dirt, can be as long as 10 feet (3 m) and as deep as 4-5 feet (1.2-1.5 m) with several chambers for sleeping, storing food and waste, may nest in tree cavity; male and female construct and maintain separate burrows

Food: omnivore; seeds, fruit, nuts, insects, fungi, buds, flowers, frogs, baby birds, bird eggs, small snakes

Sounds: very trilling "chip" note repeated over and over, lower pitched "chuck-chuck-chuck" sound may last several minutes and echo through the woods

Breeding: Mar-Apr mating; 28-30 days gestation

Young: up to 7 offspring 1-2 times a year in May or June

(more information on next page) 129

cheek pouch

burrow entrance

Signs: piles of cracked seeds and acorns and other food on a log or large rock; oblong dark brown pellets, ⅛" (.3 cm) long, often not seen and not key in identifying this species

Activity: diurnal; peak activity in the morning and evening, no activity on cold, windy or rainy days

Tracks: hind paw 1¼-1½" (3-4 cm) long with 5 toes, forepaw with 4 toes is about half the size of hind paw; 1 set of 4 tracks; hind paws fall in front of fore prints; tracks rarely seen since it lives in a dry rocky habitat and usually does not come out from burrow when snow is on the ground

Stan's Notes: Found throughout Michigan. Range extends from Minnesota east to New England and south to the Gulf coast. The Latin genus name *Tamias* means "storer" and refers to its habit of storing large amounts of food in preparation for winter.

Known for loud vocalizations, which almost always are accompanied by a dramatic flick of the tail. Both the male and female vocalize. Usually sounds off while on a favorite perch, where it can survey its territory.

Doesn't cause damage to gardens, as some may think. Its burrows actually help to aerate the ground. Consumes great quantities of seeds that would otherwise germinate in lawns and gardens.

Chipmunks are delightful to watch and many people like to feed them. Can be very tame and tolerant of people. Usually solitary and very commonly seen around human dwellings. Maintains a small territory around the main burrow and will defend it from other "chippies." Has short, dead-end burrows for quick escapes.

Will eat just about anything from plants to animals. Comfortable climbing trees to gather seeds, buds and flowers for food. Can transport large amounts of food, usually seeds, in cheek pouches. Stores large quantities of seeds, nuts and dried berries in an underground cavity connected to its living chambers. Will eat from its cache when it cannot get outside to due weather and in winter.

A light hibernator, waking every 2-3 weeks to eat its stored food. Can occasionally be seen above ground during warm spells in winter. Common to see it in February, although it usually goes back to sleep until March, when mating season begins.

Breeding season begins a few weeks after it emerges from hibernation, and lasts only a few weeks. Male emerges before female. Female can have two litters per season, but this is not common. Male takes no part in raising young.

Southern

Northern Flying Squirrel
Southern Flying Squirrel
Glaucomys sabrinus and Glaucomys volans

Northern
Southern
Both

Family: Squirrels (Sciuridae)

Size: Northern L 7-9" (18-22.5 cm); T 4-7" (10-18 cm)
Southern L 5-7" (13-18 cm); T 3-5" (7.5-13 cm)

Weight: Northern 1½-3½ oz. (43-99 g)
Southern 1½-2½ oz. (43-71 g)

Description: Light brown-to-gray fur above. White underside. Wide flat tail, gray above and white below. Large, bulging dark eyes. Loose fold of skin between front and hind legs.

Origin/Age: native; 2-5 years

Compare: Northern and Southern Flying Squirrels appear nearly identical, but differ in size and range.

Habitat: urban and suburban yards and parks; Northern: mixed woods, coniferous and deciduous forests; Southern: deciduous forests

Home: nest lined with soft plant material, usually in an old woodpecker hole, sometimes in a nest box or an attic in homes and outbuildings, may build a small round nest of leaves on a tree branch; nest is similar to that of the Eastern Gray Squirrel

Food: omnivore; seeds, nuts, carrion, baby mice, baby birds, bird eggs, lichens, mushrooms, fungi

Sounds: faint, bird-like calls during the night, young give high-pitched squeaks

Breeding: spring mating; 40 days gestation

Young: 2-6 (average 3) offspring; Northern usually has only 1 litter per year, Southern has 2 per year

(more information on next page)

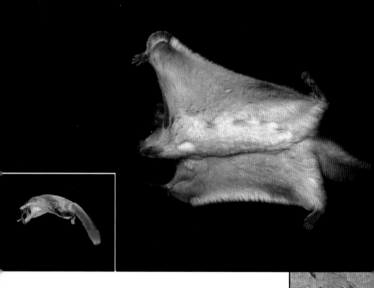

Signs: food has mysteriously disappeared from bird feeders overnight

Activity: nocturnal; active year-round, Southern sometimes enters torpor during the very coldest parts of winter

scat

Tracks: Northern hind paw 1½" (4 cm) long with 5 toes, forepaw ¾" (2 cm) long with 4 toes; Southern hind paw 1" (2.5 cm) long with 5 toes, forepaw ½" (1 cm) long with 4 toes; 1 set of 4 tracks; large landing mark (sitzmark) followed by bounding tracks, with hind paws falling in front of front prints; tracks lead to the base of a tree or suddenly appear in snow

Stan's Notes: The flying squirrel is the only nocturnal member of the Squirrel family in Michigan. Its large bulging eyes enable it to see well at night. Common name "Flying Squirrel" is a misnomer because this animal does not have the capability to fly, only the ability to glide. In part, this is due to a large flap of skin (patagium) attached to its front and hind legs and sides of its body.

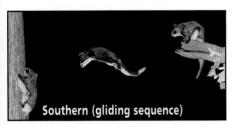

Southern (gliding sequence)

To glide, a flying squirrel will climb to the top of a tree and launch itself, extending its four legs outward and stretching the patagium to make a flat, wing-like airfoil. Its flat tail adds some additional lift and acts like a rudder to help maneuver objects while gliding. Most glides are as long as 20-50 feet (6.1-15.2 m) and terminate at the trunk of another tree. To create an air brake for a soft landing, the squirrel will quickly lift its head and tuck its tail between its hind legs. After landing, it will scamper to the opposite side of the tree trunk, presumably to avoid any flying predators that may be following.

The flying squirrel is the most carnivorous of the tree squirrels, finding, killing and eating small mice, dead flesh (carrion) and even baby birds and bird eggs. It is a gregarious animal, with many individuals living together in a nest.

Young are born helpless with eyes closed. Weaned at 5-7 weeks, they may stay with their mother through their first winter.

Most flying squirrels live only 2-5 years, but some have lived as long as 10 years in captivity. However, please don't capture these animals. While the Northern is less aggressive than the Southern, neither makes a good pet.

Thirteen-lined Ground Squirrel
Ictidomys tridecemlineatus

Family: Squirrels (Sciuridae)

Size: L 6-8" (15-20 cm); T 2-5" (5-13 cm)

Weight: 4-9 oz. (113-255 g)

Description: Long narrow brown body with 13 alternating tan and dark brown stripes from nape to base of tail. Small tan spots in the dark stripes. Short round ears. Large dark eyes. Short legs. Thin hairy tail, one-third the length of body.

Origin/Age: native; 1-3 years

Compare: Similar size as Eastern Chipmunk (pg. 129), but has smaller ears and more stripes, with tan spots on dark stripes.

Habitat: fields, lawns, pastures, meadows, prairies, along roads, cemeteries

Home: burrow, up to 20 feet (6.1 m) long and often only several feet deep, with a hibernation chamber beneath the frost line and no excess dirt at the entrance, many side tunnels and several entrance and exit holes; will plug entrances and exits each night with plant material

Food: omnivore; green plants, seeds, insects, bird eggs, baby mice

Sounds: trill-like whistles when threatened or alarmed

Breeding: usually April mating; 27-28 days gestation

Young: 6-12 offspring once per year in May; born naked with eyes closed, becomes independent after it is weaned, seen above ground by about 6 weeks

(more information on next page)

juveniles

Signs: small round entrance holes in the grass, runways 2 inches (5 cm) wide worn in grass (made by its low-slung body and short legs) leading to and from the holes; scat is rarely seen since the animal often defecates in its burrow or in tall grass

Activity: diurnal; most active a couple of hours after sunrise and through midday, retires to its burrow 1-2 hours before sunset, does not come out on cold, windy or rainy days, rarely comes out when snow is on the ground

Tracks: hind paw 1½" (4 cm) long with 5 toes, forepaw 1" (2.5 cm) long with 4 toes; tracks usually seen around burrow entrance

Stan's Notes: Not a gopher, but sometimes called Striped Gopher. Also called Federation Squirrel due to the pattern of stripes with spots on its body that resemble the U.S. Stars and Stripes.

When there is frequent human contact at places such as roadside rest areas and golf courses, it can be friendly and is usually tame. Semi-social, interacting with other ground squirrels during the day when feeding. Individuals have separate burrows, but live in large colonies. Colonies are not highly organized and may result from a reduction in available habitat.

A fast runner, reaching speeds up to 8 miles (13 km) per hour. Zigzags and turns back when pursued. Stands upright to survey its territory. Gives a trill-like whistle at the first sign of danger and runs quickly to the main burrow or into one of its short, dead-end escape burrows. Often stays inside the entrance, poking its head out, repeating its alarm call.

Stores some seeds in burrow for cold or rainy days. When insects are abundant, eats more insects than plants. Adds enough body fat in summer to start hibernating in September or October. Often enters hibernation sooner than chipmunks and emerges later, making it one of the longest true hibernators in Michigan. Does not wake to feed, like chipmunks. Rolls up into a ball in the hibernation chamber. Heart rate, body temperature and respiration drop dramatically. Reduced heart rate and respiration conserve energy in winter, but still loses up to half its body weight by spring.

Male emerges from hibernation before female. Mating occurs just after female emerges, usually in April. The short breeding season may explain why the female has only one litter each year. After mating, the male does not participate in raising young.

Young often do not disperse far, and dig their own burrows near their mother. This substantially increases the colony size.

Red Squirrel
Tamiasciurus hudsonicus

Family: Squirrels (Sciuridae)

Size: L 7-9" (18-22.5 cm); T 4-7" (10-18 cm)

Weight: 5-9 oz. (142-255 g)

Description: Overall rusty red, with brighter red fur on sides. Bright white belly. Distinctive white ring around eyes. Large, fluffy red tail with a black tip. Black line separating the red back from the white belly in summer. Tufted ears in winter.

Origin/Age: native; 2-5 years

Compare: The smallest and the only red tree squirrel.

Habitat: coniferous and deciduous forests, suburban and urban yards, parks

Home: nest (drey) made mainly with strips of grapevine bark and dried leaves, in a tree cavity or sometimes in a burrow, may make a small ball-shaped nest from lichen and grass, may take over the leaf nest of an Eastern Gray Squirrel

Food: omnivore; pine cone seeds and other seeds, nuts, fruit, acorns, corn, mushrooms; also eats baby birds, bird eggs and carrion

Sounds: loud raspy chatters or wheezy barks when upset or threatened by people or animals (including other squirrels), may bark nonstop for up to an hour, distinctive buzz-like calls given by the male when chasing a female to mate

Breeding: Feb-Mar mating; 33-35 days gestation

Young: 2-5 offspring once per year from March to May; born naked with eyes closed, weaned and on its own after 7-8 weeks

(more information on next page) 141

Isle Royale

drying mushrooms

scat

Signs: discarded pine cone parts (midden) in a pile on the ground under a tree branch, acorns and other large nuts with a single ragged hole at one end and nutmeat missing

Activity: diurnal; active year-round, but may hole up for a couple days in the nest during very cold, hot or rainy weather

Tracks: hind paw 1½" (4 cm) long with 5 toes, forepaw ¾" (2 cm) long with 4 toes; 1 set of 4 tracks; forepaws fall side by side and behind hind prints

Stan's Notes: Although it may be small, the Red Squirrel has a very big attitude and is well known for chasing away the larger Eastern Gray Squirrel or any other small mammal. However, the success of the Red Squirrel over the Gray is a function of the food resources, not its feistiness.

Very common in non-coniferous habitats, but usually associated with pine trees. Feeds heavily on pine cone seeds. Cuts the cones from trees and carries them to a specific spot to eat. A large pile of discarded cone parts, known as a midden, accumulates under the perch. Caches up to a bushel of fresh cones in the midden to eat later. Large middens are usually the result of several squirrels using the same favorite perch over time, with one taking over the spot when another dies. Consumes Amanita mushrooms, which are poisonous to humans, without ill effects. Hangs mushrooms to dry on tree branches for future consumption.

Like the Gray, it constructs leaf nests (dreys), but does not build as many. Dreys are built closer to the main trunk with more sticks and less leaves and are half the size of Gray Squirrel nests.

Several males will chase a female on tree branches prior to mating. A male may mate with more than one female, but the female is receptive to mating only once on one day in late winter or spring.

The most seasonally dimorphic of squirrels, molting in late spring and again in early autumn. Black morph and white albinos occur but are quite uncommon, unlike other squirrel species.

The genus *Tamiasciurus* is only in North America and includes one other species, Douglas Squirrel, which occurs in the Pacific Northwest. The species name *hudsonicus* was given because the Red Squirrel ranges as far north in Canada to Hudson Bay and west across Canada and most of Alaska. In fact, it has one of the widest distributions of any squirrel in North America. Due to long-term isolation from the mainland population, a unique sub-species of Red Squirrel is found on Isle Royale in Lake Superior.

Eastern Gray Squirrel
Sciurus carolinensis

Family: Squirrels (Sciuridae)

Size: L 9-10" (22.5-25 cm); T 8-9" (20-22.5 cm)

Weight: ¾-1½ lb. (.3-.7 kg)

Description: Overall gray or light brown fur with a white chest and belly. Large, bushy gray tail with silver-tipped hairs. Black morph is overall black with a reddish brown shine. Tail may also be reddish brown.

Origin/Age: native; 2-5 years

Compare: Smaller than the Eastern Fox Squirrel (pg. 149), which has a rusty orange tail. Larger than the Red Squirrel (pg. 141), which is red.

Habitat: woodlands, suburban and urban yards, parks

Home: leaf nest (drey) in summer, hollow with a single entrance hole and lined with soft plant material, nest is in a tree cavity or old woodpecker hole in winter; male and female live in separate nests in summer, but together in winter

Food: omnivore; nuts, seeds, birdseed, fruit, corn, leaf buds, flowers, mushrooms, inner tree bark, baby birds, bird eggs, mice and other small mammals, insects, carrion

Sounds: hoarse, wheezy calls repeated many times when upset or threatened, chatters as an alarm call to warn of predators such as a house cat

Breeding: Jan-Feb mating; 40-45 days gestation

Young: 2-6 offspring once (sometimes twice) per year; born naked with eyes closed, eyes open at about 5 weeks, weaned at about 8-9 weeks, mother will push young away shortly after weaning

(more information on next page) 145

albino

black morph

Signs: acorns and other large nuts split in half with the nutmeat missing, gnaw marks on tree branches stripped of bark, trees that lack new growth branches with green leaves in early summer, ragged holes in snow with scattered dirt and debris (from recovery of buried acorns)

scat

Activity: diurnal; active year-round, feeds late in morning and throughout the day, often rests a couple hours in the afternoon, may stay in nest for several days during very cold or hot periods

Tracks: hind paw 2¼" (5.5 cm) long with 5 toes, forepaw 1" (2.5 cm) long with 4 toes; 1 set of 4 tracks; forepaws fall side by side and behind hind prints

Stan's Notes: The most commonly seen mammal in Michigan, it hardly needs a description. The black morph is born black and stays black. Pockets of black morph squirrels occur throughout the state. The albino morph, which is entirely white with pink eyes, is more rare and does not live as long as the black morph.

Spends most of its life in trees, going to the ground only to feed on fallen nuts and seeds. Buries large amounts of nuts, most only ¼ inch (.6 cm) underground. Studies show about 85 percent of these nuts are recovered. Nuts buried by scientists were recovered at a similar rate, indicating that squirrels find buried food by the sense of smell, not memory. Able to locate nuts even beneath deep snow. Many squirrels "migrate" in years with poor nut crops, moving to find a new home range with an adequate food supply.

During the mating season, males will chase the females. Mating chases are long, with much jumping, bounding and biting.

Leaf nests (dreys) are located away from the main trunk of a tree and are constructed to shed water. A squirrel can have up to seven dreys, which are sometimes used as emergency nests. Usually born in a cavity nest, babies may be moved to a drey when the mother feels threatened. Mothers raise their young alone and move them from nest to nest, perhaps to avoid flea infestations. Studies show that 80 percent die in their first year due to predation by animals that eat squirrels such as coyotes, foxes and hawks.

leaf nest

Considered a nuisance by many because it eats birdseed. Eats a variety of foods, however, including some mushrooms that are poisonous to humans. Famous for its ability to access nearly any bird feeder, spending hours, days or weeks devising a way to get the food. An industry has flourished around squirrel-proof feeders.

Eastern Fox Squirrel
Sciurus niger

Family: Squirrels (Sciuridae)

Size: L 10-15" (25-38 cm); T 8-13" (20-33 cm)

Weight: 1-2¼ lb. (.5-1 kg)

Description: Dark gray fur with yellow and orange highlights. Bright rusty orange chin, chest and belly. Large, fluffy, rusty orange tail. Very rare black morph has a white nose and belly and white-tipped ears.

Origin/Age: native; 2-5 years

Compare: The Eastern Gray Squirrel (pg. 145) is smaller, lacks a rusty orange tail and is more common.

Habitat: woodlands, suburban and urban yards, parks

Home: leaf nest (drey) in summer, up to 2 feet (61 cm) wide, lined with soft plant material, usually with a side entrance, in a major fork near the main trunk of a tree, nest is in a tree cavity in winter and occupied by several individuals if enough food is available, also used for birthing; may build and use up to 6 nests

Food: omnivore; nuts, corn, pine cone seeds and other seeds, fruit, mushrooms, bird eggs, baby birds, mice, insects, carrion

Sounds: scolding calls similar to those of the Eastern Gray Squirrel, only more hoarse

Breeding: Jan-Feb mating; 40-45 days gestation

Young: 2-4 offspring 1-2 times per year; born with eyes closed, eyes open at about 30 days, leaves mother and on own at about 3 months

(more information on next page) 149

Signs: large debris pile of split nutshells, whole corncobs and husks strewn about underneath the feeding perch

Activity: diurnal; active year-round, usually begins feeding late in the morning, several hours after sunrise, often active during the middle of the day

Tracks: hind paw 2¾-3" (7-7.5 cm) long with 5 toes, forepaw 1½" (4 cm) long with 4 toes; 1 set of 4 tracks; forepaws fall side by side and behind hind prints

Stan's Notes: The largest of tree squirrels, with its bright rusty orange color making it easy to spot in the forest. Common name "Fox" was given for its oversized rusty orange tail, which is like that of the Red Fox. Some individuals are black with a white nose and belly and white-tipped ears, hence the species name *niger*.

Eastern Gray Squirrels often outnumber Eastern Fox Squirrels in areas where they both occur, but Eastern Fox Squirrels appear slightly more dominant. Compared with Eastern Gray Squirrels, Fox Squirrels spend more time farther away from trees, searching for food on the ground and traveling, but they both collect, bury and retrieve nuts in the same way, using the sense of smell to find buried nuts. Unlike Gray Squirrels, Fox Squirrels carry food back to a "regular" spot to eat. While Gray Squirrels use nearly all available tree cavities for their nests, Fox Squirrels build large leaf nests in crotches of trees.

leaf nest

Eastern Fox Squirrels have a large home range of up to 50 acres (20 ha), which is ten times larger than the range of Eastern Gray Squirrels, so only a few individuals are seen in any given area. While they are very similar to the Gray Squirrel in diet and habits, Fox Squirrels have a limited distribution, often faring better in small isolated woodlands with a good supply of corn nearby.

Fox Squirrels are rarely found to have tapeworms or roundworms upon examination of stomach contents. One explanation is the acorns they eat contain large amounts of tannin, which is highly toxic to these parasites.

Several males "chase" one female prior to mating, following her throughout the day. Female will mate with more than one male.

Woodchuck
Marmota monax

Family: Squirrels (Sciuridae)

Size: L 18-28" (45-71 cm); T 3-6" (7.5-15 cm)

Weight: 4-14 lb. (1.8-6.3 kg)

Description: Various shades of red to brown or gray to black. Hair is tipped with gray, yellow or black, giving it a salt-and-pepper appearance. A wide body with very short legs. Small round ears. Dark eyes. Dark brown or black feet. Large, bushy dark tail. Male slightly larger than female.

Origin/Age: native; 2-4 years

Compare: Much larger than Thirteen-lined Ground Squirrel (pg. 137), with a wider body. The wide body and short legs make the Woodchuck easy to identify.

Habitat: fields, pastures, meadows, around homes and other buildings, woodland edges, woodlands

Home: den, often underneath a building or steps, up to 30 feet (9.1 m) long and down to 5 feet (1.5 m) deep; entrance is 8-12 inches (20-30 cm) wide, often with large dirt piles outside, almost always has 1-2 additional escape entrances, which don't have dirt piles

Food: herbivore; green vegetation, leaf buds, grasses; especially likes dandelions

Sounds: sharp, whistle-like alarm call

Breeding: Mar-Apr mating; 30 days gestation

Young: 3-7 offspring once per year in May or June; born naked with eyes closed, opens eyes and crawls at about 4 weeks, weaned at about 6 weeks, will disperse to own area at 8-10 weeks

(more information on next page) 153

Signs: wide holes underneath buildings and in hillsides, leaves and flowers that have been chewed off neatly; small, round brown pellets, ¼-½" (.6-1 cm) wide, deposited into special underground chambers

Activity: diurnal; most active in the morning and evening, especially during the hot summer months, spends many hours feeding on grass

Tracks: hind paw 3-3¾" (7.5-9.5 cm) long with 5 toes, forepaw with 4 toes is slightly smaller than hind paw; tracks are not very common since the animal does not come out when there is snow on the ground, when conditions are muddy or in wet weather

Stan's Notes: The Woodchuck is a type of marmot and is the largest member of the Squirrel family in Michigan. The common name "Woodchuck" is said to come from the Cree Indian word *wuchak*, which was used to describe several small brown animals. The animal for which Groundhog Day is named, it is also known as Groundhog or Whistle Pig. These common names come from its stout stature and sharp whistle-like call it gives when alarmed.

Solitary except for mating and when a mother raises her young. All other marmots, most of which occur in western states, are colonial. It is rarely seen feeding far from the den entrance, since retreating into the den is its major line of defense. Will wait at the entrance until danger has passed, then slowly returns to feeding. Unlike the common name suggests, the Woodchuck does not eat wood, but feeds instead on green vegetation such as grass and especially likes dandelions. Will climb small trees in spring to eat the green buds.

juvenile

Feeds during the summer, adding body fat to sustain it through hibernation. Will lay curled up in a ball with its head between its front legs. A true hibernator, its body temperature drops from 90°F (32°C) to 40°F (4°C), breathing slows to only once every 6 minutes and heart rate decreases from 75 to 4 beats per minute.

Has a large tunnel system, which is often used by other mammals such as cottontails, raccoons and opossums. Usually will have separate summer and winter dens. The winter den is often in a woodland. It has a single entrance, and the hibernation chamber is lined with dried grass and leaves.

The female Woodchuck breeds at 1 year of age. She may use a separate chamber in the den to give birth.

Least Weasel
Mustela nivalis

Family: Weasels and Skunks (Mustelidae)

Size: L 6-7" (15-18 cm); T ¾-1¼" (2-3 cm)

Weight: 1-2 oz. (28-57 g)

Description: Light to dark brown with a brown tail and white chin, throat, chest, belly and feet in the summer. Small, thin tubular body. Short legs and tail. All white in winter.

Origin/Age: native; 3-7 years

Compare: Smaller than the Long-tailed Weasel (pg. 165), which has a white-to-yellow underside and long black-tipped tail. Short-tailed Weasel (pg. 161) is larger and has a longer tail that is black-tipped. Look for the Least Weasel's short all-brown tail in summer or all-white body and tail in winter.

Habitat: fields, wetlands, prairies, farms

Home: burrow, often an old chipmunk burrow, hollow log or crevice underneath a rock pile; has several burrows in its territory

Food: carnivore, insectivore; small mammals such as voles, mice and moles; also eats small birds, bird eggs and insects

Sounds: occasional loud shrills, hisses when threatened

Breeding: year-round mating; 34-37 days gestation; unlike the other weasels, implantation is not delayed

Young: 1-6 offspring up to 3 times per year

(more information on next page)

Signs: long, thin, nearly black scat, contains the hair and bones of voles and mice

Activity: diurnal, nocturnal; hunts for several hours, then rests and sleeps for several hours

Tracks: forepaw and hind paw ½" (1 cm) long, round with well-defined nail marks, 5 toes on all feet; 1 set of 4 tracks when bounding; 8-10" (20-25 cm) stride

Stan's Notes: The smallest of weasels, uncommon and seldom seen. Solitary most of the year, except for mating. Excellent sight, hearing and sense of smell. Can climb trees, but spends most of its time on the ground. Runs up to 6 miles (10 km) per hour on flat ground. Often stands on hind legs to get a better look around.

Fast, agile and small enough to follow its favorite food, Meadow Voles, or mice into tunnels. Kills with a single bite to the base of the skull to sever the spinal cord. Can eat up to 40 percent of its own weight in food every day. Sometimes kills more than it can eat and caches the extra.

winter

Like other weasels, it emits a strong pungent odor from glands near the base of its tail when excited or threatened. Also uses this scent to mark territory.

Male occupies a small territory of 2 acres (.8 ha). Female territory is even smaller.

Male becomes sexually active at 8 months. Female matures at 4 months, but rarely breeds during the year of her birth.

winter

Short-tailed Weasel
Mustela erminea

Family: Weasels and Skunks (Mustelidae)

Size: L 7-10" (18-25 cm); T 2-4" (5-10 cm)

Weight: 2-6 oz. (57-170 g)

Description: Light to dark brown with a black-tipped brown tail and white chin, throat, chest, belly and feet in summer. Long, thin tubular body. Short legs. White in winter with a black-tipped tail. Male is slightly larger than female.

Origin/Age: native; 3-7 years

Compare: Smaller than Mink (pg. 173), which has a white patch on the chin and lacks a white throat, chest and belly. Long-tailed Weasel (pg. 165) is also all white in winter with a black-tipped tail, but has a white-to-yellow underside in summer.

Habitat: open mixed forests, wetlands, prairies, farms

Home: burrow, often an old chipmunk burrow; several burrows scattered in its territory

Food: carnivore, insectivore; small to medium mammals such as mice, voles, chipmunks, rabbits and Red Squirrels; also eats insects

Sounds: loud chatters, piercing shrills, hisses if threatened

Breeding: summer (July) mating; 27-28 days gestation; implantation is delayed up to 8-9 months after mating

Young: 4-9 offspring once per year

(more information on next page)

changing color

Signs: long thin scat with a pointed end, often contains hair and bones

Activity: primarily nocturnal, diurnal mostly in winter; hunts during the day for several hours, then rests and sleeps for several hours

scat

Tracks: hind paw ¾-1" (2-2.5 cm) long, forepaw slightly smaller, both round with well-defined nail marks, 5 toes on all feet; 1 set of 4 tracks when bounding; 10-12" (25-30 cm) stride

Stan's Notes: This is a small weasel with a big attitude, capturing and killing animals several times its own weight. Chases, pounces, then kills prey with one bite to the base of the skull, severing the spinal cord. Like other weasels, usually laps up blood from prey before eating it, giving rise to the myth that the weasel kills just to suck blood from its victims. Occasionally catches and kills more than it can eat and caches the extra food.

Always on the move, hunting mostly on the ground, but can climb trees. Excellent sight and smell. Rarely seen more than one at a time except when the female is teaching her offspring to hunt.

winter

Male has a larger territory than the female. Matures sexually in the second year. Male drags the female around by the scruff of the neck during mating, which may last several hours. Males mating with mothers that have offspring may also mate with their female young.

Female matures sexually the summer of her first year. Usually the female raises the young by herself, but there are some reports of the male helping. Offspring are taught to hunt by 6-10 weeks.

Also known as Stoat during summer, when the animal is brown. Like the Long-tailed Weasel, it is referred to as Ermine during the winter, when it is all white.

Long-tailed Weasel
Mustela frenata

Family: Weasels and Skunks (Mustelidae)

Size: L 8-16" (20-40 cm); T 3-6" (7.5-15 cm)

Weight: 3-9 oz. (85-255 g)

Description: Light brown in summer with a long black-tipped brown tail, brown feet and white-to-yellow chin, throat, chest and belly. Long tubular body. Short legs. White in the winter with a black-tipped tail. Male slightly larger than female.

Origin/Age: native; 5-10 years

Compare: Larger than Short-tailed Weasel (pg. 161), which has a shorter tail and white feet. Mink (pg. 173) is larger, darker brown with a white patch on the chin and doesn't turn white during winter. Much larger than the Least Weasel (pg. 157), which has a very short tail that lacks a black tip.

Habitat: mixed forests, fields, wetlands, prairies, farms

Home: abandoned burrows, usually chipmunk, ground squirrel and mole burrows; often has several in its territory

Food: carnivore, insectivore; small to medium mammals such as voles, mice, chipmunks, squirrels and rabbits; will also eat small birds, bird eggs, carrion and insects

Sounds: single loud trills or rapid trills, squeals

Breeding: summer (July) mating; 30-34 days gestation; ova develop for 8 days after fertilization, then cease development, implantation is delayed up to 8-10 months after mating

Young: 4-8 offspring once per year in spring

(more information on next page) 165

Signs: long, thin, often dark scat with a pointed end, contains hair and bones, often on a log or rock, very similar to mink scat

Activity: primarily nocturnal, diurnal mostly during the winter; hunts during the day for several hours, then rests and sleeps for several hours

Tracks: hind paw ¾-1" (2-2.5 cm) long, forepaw slightly smaller, both round with well-defined nail marks, 5 toes on all feet; 1 set of 4 tracks when bounding; 12-20" (30-50 cm) stride

Stan's Notes: This is a very active predator that runs in a series of bounds with back arched and tail elevated. A good swimmer and can climb trees in pursuit of squirrels. Quickly locates prey using its excellent eyesight and sense of smell, dashes to grab it, then kills it with several bites to the base of the skull. Favorite foods are Meadow Voles and Deer Mice. Usually hunts for larger prey such as rabbits. Eats its fill and caches the rest. Consumes 25-40 percent of its own body weight in food daily.

Male maintains a territory of 25-55 acres (10-22 ha). Territory of the female is smaller. Both apply a smelly, oily substance secreted by glands located near the base of the tail to rocks and trees to mark territorial boundaries. Can be seen applying the substance, but the odor is rarely detectible to humans, especially after a few days. Will defend territory against other weasels. Solitary except during the mating season and when a mother is with her young.

winter

American Marten
Martes americana

Family: Weasels and Skunks (Mustelidae)

Size: L 12-21" (30-53 cm); T 5-9" (13-22.5 cm); H 6-7" (15-18 cm)

Weight: 1-4 lb. (.5-1.8 kg)

Description: Body ranges from light brown to nearly blond or dark brown to nearly black. Head is lighter in color than the body, usually gray to nearly white. Large ears and short snout. Light orange or buff throat patch. Long bushy tail. Male slightly larger than female.

Origin/Age: native; 5-15 years

Compare: Smaller than Fisher (pg. 177), which is darker and lacks the orange throat patch. Similar size as Mink (pg. 173), which has a white patch on the chin and a thin dark-tipped tail.

Habitat: coniferous forests, wetlands

Home: burrow, often a hollow log or tree or rock crevice, may use an old squirrel nest or woodpecker hole

Food: omnivore; small mammals such as mice, voles, squirrels, chipmunks and rabbits; also eats birds, eggs, berries, insects, earthworms and pine seeds

Sounds: snarls and hisses when threatened, various huffs and screams during mating

Breeding: midsummer mating; 26-27 days gestation; implantation is delayed up to 6-8 months after mating

Young: 2-5 (usually 2) offspring once per year in March or April; born naked with eyes closed, weaned at 5-6 weeks, nearly adult size at about 90 days

(more information on next page) 169

Signs: small, dark and often thin scat, usually containing hair and bones, seen at scat stations where droppings are repeatedly deposited, used to mark territory, closely resembles mink scat

Activity: diurnal, nocturnal; active year-round, especially on overcast days

Tracks: hind paw 1½-1¾" (4-4.5 cm) long, forepaw slightly smaller; 1 set of 4 tracks when bounding; 6-8" (15-20 cm) stride, sometimes has a tail drag mark; tracks may be seen in snow, often leading to and from trees

Stan's Notes: An excellent tree climber, also called Pine Marten because of its close association with coniferous forests. Its thick fur makes it well suited to life in a snowy environment. A strong swimmer, even underwater. Like others in the Weasel family, it often has a musky odor. Very vocal when encountering another marten, snarling and baring its teeth.

Diet consists of more than 100 types of food, nearly all of it meat. Prefers Red and Gray Squirrels, frequently taking over their nests after killing and eating them. Looks much like a squirrel when searching on the ground for voles.

The male has a home range of 5-15 square miles (13-39 sq. km). Female range is smaller.

Much play and wrestling during courtship, which lasts as long as a couple weeks. Breeds with several mates (polygamous) each season.

Female matures sexually at 15 months and scent marks to advertise she is receptive to mating. Mother marten often leaves her young after weaning them, and mates again.

Habitat destruction has led to a sharp decrease in the population over the past century. A solitary, inquisitive species. Some people can attract martens to their yards by setting out raw chicken.

Mink
Neovison vison

Family: Weasels and Skunks (Mustelidae)

Size: L 14-20" (36-50 cm); T 6-8" (15-20 cm)

Weight: 1½-3½ lb. (0.7-1.6 kg)

Description: Dark brown to nearly black or brown to blond, often with a luster. Short, round dark ears. Small white patch on the chin. Long tubular body with short legs. A long bushy tail, darker near the tip. Male slightly larger than female.

Origin/Age: native; 5-10 years

Compare: Larger than Long-tailed Weasel (pg. 165), which is lighter brown with white-to-yellow underside. Much larger than Short-tailed Weasel (pg. 161), which has a shorter tail and white underside. Mink does not turn white in winter.

Habitat: along rivers, lakes and streams, wetlands, farms, forests

Home: burrow, entrance width is 4 inches (10 cm)

Food: carnivore; small to medium mammals such as voles, mice, chipmunks, rabbits and squirrels, but favors muskrats; also eats small birds, bird eggs, snakes, frogs, toads, crayfish and fish

Sounds: chatters, scolds, hisses, snarls when alarmed or fighting other minks

Breeding: Jan-Apr mating; 32-51 days gestation; implantation delayed, length of delay is dependent upon when the female mates during the season

Young: 3-6 offspring once per year; born covered with fine hair and eyes closed, eyes open at about 7 weeks, weaned at 8-9 weeks, mature at 5 months

(more information on next page) 173

brown morph

Signs: small, thin dark scat, usually pointed at one end, usually containing bone, fur and fish scales, deposited on rocks and logs along lakes and rivers

scat

Activity: nocturnal, diurnal; hunts for several hours, then rests several hours

Tracks: hind paw 2-3¼" (5-8 cm) long with 5 toes, forepaw 1¼-1¾" (3-4.5 cm) long with 5 toes, both round with well-defined nail marks; 1 set of 4 tracks when bounding; 12-25" (30-63 cm) stride; tracks may end at the edge of water

Stan's Notes: Also known as the American Mink. Usually seen along the banks of rivers and lakes. Its thick, oily, waterproof fur provides great insulation and enables the animal to swim in nearly freezing water. Its partially webbed toes aid in swimming. Can swim as far as 100 feet (30 m) underwater before surfacing. Able to dive down to 15 feet (4.5 m) for one of its favorite foods, muskrats.

Hunts on land for chipmunks, rabbits, snakes and frogs. Moves in a series of loping bounds with its back arched and tail held out slightly above horizontal. When frightened or excited, releases an odorous substance from glands near the base of its tail.

Burrow is almost always near water, often under a tree root or in a riverbank. May use a hollow log or muskrat burrow after killing and eating the occupants. Active burrows will often have a strong odor near the entrance. Most burrows are temporary since minks are almost constantly on the move looking for their next meal.

The male maintains a territory of up to 40 acres (16 ha), with the female territory less than half the size. Will mark its territory by applying a pungent discharge on prominent rocks and logs. It is a polygamous breeder.

The pelt of a mink is considered to be one of the most luxurious. Demand for the fur has led to the establishment of mink ranches, where the fur color can be controlled by selective breeding.

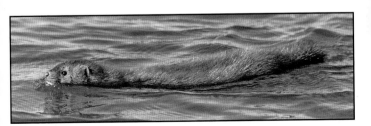

Fisher
Martes pennanti

Family: Weasels and Skunks (Mustelidae)

Size: L 20-24" (50-60 cm); T 11-17" (28-43 cm); H 7-9" (18-22.5 cm)

Weight: 4-18 lb. (1.8-8.1 kg)

Description: Long soft fur, overall dark brown. Narrow snout. Short round ears. Large round feet and long sharp claws. A very long bushy tail, often darker than the body. Male slightly larger than female.

Origin/Age: native; 5-15 years

Compare: Larger than American Marten (pg. 169), which is lighter brown and has an orange throat patch. Much larger than Mink (pg. 173), which has a white patch on chin and thin tail with a dark tip. Fisher has a longer muzzle than other weasels.

Habitat: mature coniferous forests with closed canopies, mature mixed forests, wetlands

Home: no regular den; constantly on the move

Food: carnivore; small to medium mammals such as mice, chipmunks, ground squirrels, porcupines and hares; also eats carrion; less often eats eggs, berries, nuts, plants and apples

Sounds: loud chuckles and purr-like noises when content, growls when threatened or during mating

Breeding: late winter (Mar-Apr) mating; 28-30 days gestation; implantation delayed up to 10-11 months after mating

Young: 1-6 offspring once per year, born with fine hair and eyes and ears closed, eyes open at about 7 weeks, leaves den at 12-14 weeks

(more information on next page) 177

juvenile

Signs: dark cylindrical scat, segmented with a pointed end, usually containing fur, bones and porcupine quill fragments

Activity: nocturnal, diurnal; active night and day, usually hunts up to 4-5 hours, then sleeps several hours

scat

Tracks: forepaw and hind paw 2-3" (5-7.5 cm) long, round with well-defined nail marks, 5 toes on all feet; 1 set of 4 tracks when bounding; 10-20" (25-50 cm) stride; tracks may end at a tree or lead to and from trees

Stan's Notes: Unique to North America. Once found throughout Michigan, but was nearly extirpated because of trapping and logging. Now returning mostly to the Upper Peninsula.

The largest member of the Weasel family. The common name is a misnomer because it does not fish. Perhaps the name came from people mistaking it for its smaller cousin, the Mink, which is a good fisher. Once called American Sable due to its long soft fur.

Like other weasels, the Fisher has a musky odor. Has retractable (retractile) claws like cats. It is a solitary animal, strong swimmer and tree climber. One of the few animals that will routinely kill and eat porcupines and rarely sustain an injury. Prefers forests with a high closed canopy.

Except for expectant mothers, does not have a regular den since it is constantly moving about. Will use a hollow log or trunk, or an old squirrel or hawk nest for short periods. Sleeps on a large tree branch high above ground in warm weather. Uses a natural cavity in a tree or an underground mammal den for resting or holing up for a couple days during bad weather in winter.

The male Fisher has a large territory of 50-150 square miles (130-390 sq. km), which overlaps with other male territories and at least one female territory.

Female is either pregnant or lactating nearly her entire adult life, since she mates again just days after giving birth. Female gives birth to young in a tree cavity high above ground.

American Badger
Taxidea taxus

Family: Weasels and Skunks (Mustelidae)

Size: L 20-30" (50-76 cm); T 3-6" (7.5-15 cm)

Weight: 8-25 lb. (3.6-11.3 kg)

Description: Coarse, grizzled gray upper and yellowish brown underside. A dark snout with a distinctive white stripe from the nose upward, between the eyes and to the nape. White cheeks and ears. Large wide body. Short powerful legs with long, sharp nonretractable (nonretractile) nails on front feet. Small gray tail. Male larger than female.

Origin/Age: native; 3-10 years

Compare: Larger than Woodchuck (pg. 153), which lacks the white stripe and has a large, nearly black tail.

Habitat: along roads, fields, prairies, farmlands, woodland edges

Home: large den, often in a road embankment or grassy hillside, digs its own, may overtake and enlarge a woodchuck den; uses den for birthing, raising young and during torpor

Food: carnivore, insectivore; small mammals such as voles, mice, chipmunks, rabbits and ground squirrels; also eats small birds, bird eggs, snakes, frogs, toads and insects

Sounds: loud snarls and growls

Breeding: Jul-Aug mating; 30-40 days gestation; implantation delayed until February after mating

Young: 1-5 offspring once per year in March or April; born covered with fine fur and eyes closed, eyes open at about 4 weeks, weaned at about 8 weeks

(more information on next page) 181

den entrance

scat

Signs: large pile of unearthed dirt in front of den entrance, can be seen from a great distance, bones, uneaten body parts and scat frequently scattered near the den entrance; long thin scat, segmented, often dark, contains hair and bones

Activity: nocturnal; usually does not leave den until well after dark to hunt for small mammals, occasionally leaves den during the day

Tracks: forepaw and hind paw 2" (5 cm) long and wide, round with narrow pad, separate nail marks, 5 distinct toes on all feet; fore and hind prints fall near each other when walking, 6-12" (15-30 cm) stride

Stan's Notes: The least weasel-like of weasels. Uniquely shaped, its wide flattened body, short powerful legs and narrow snout make it well suited to burrow and live underground. Has second eyelids (nictitating membranes), which protect its eyes while it digs. Uses its long, sharp front claws to dig through coarse rocky soil, expelling dirt between its hind legs like a dog. Can dig fast enough to capture ground squirrels and moles while they are still in their burrows. Has an excellent sense of smell. Believed to be able to determine just by the scent of a burrow whether or not it is occupied.

Secretive and avoids contact with people. Has the reputation of being aggressive, especially a mother defending her young. Very vocal when threatened, snarling and growling loudly.

Hunts cooperatively with coyotes. While a badger excavates one tunnel entrance, a coyote will wait for the occupant to emerge at an auxiliary escape tunnel. Frequently the coyote will chase the occupant back down the burrow to the waiting badger.

It is not a true hibernator, but enters a condition called torpor that resembles hibernation, during which the body temperature falls approximately 10°F (-12°C) and heart rate and respiration decrease to approximately half the normal rate. Torpor lasts only 20-30 hours at a time. Badgers remain awake for up to 24 hours between periods of torpor, during which time body temperature and heart rate return to normal. Because of this energy-saving torpor cycle, the body rarely uses up its stored fat by spring.

Male has a large home range, where several females also may live. Lacks a family structure. Male stays solitary while female raises young on her own. Young stay with the mother until their first autumn, when they are fully grown and can hunt on their own.

Wolverine
Gulo gulo

Rare

Family: Weasels and Skunks (Mustelidae)

Size: L 25-36" (63-90 cm); T 6-10" (15-25 cm)

Weight: 18-38 lb. (8.1-17.1 kg)

Description: Dark brown with 2 yellowish brown bands along sides from shoulders to base of tail. Broad head, light brown ears, dark muzzle. Large body. Full furry tail, darker at tip. Male is 10 percent larger than female.

Origin/Age: native; 5-10 years

Compare: Larger than American Badger (pg. 181), which has distinct white markings on head and much shorter legs. Fisher (pg. 177) is smaller, has a narrower body and lacks the yellowish bands.

Habitat: forests, along lakes and streams, prairies

Home: den, under a large rock or beneath the roots of a fallen tree, in a crevice or cave, female will dig a snow cave in higher elevations; used for birthing and raising young

Food: carnivore; medium to large mammals such as squirrels, hares, woodchucks, skunks, foxes, porcupines and deer; also eats carrion

Sounds: generally quiet, will snort, growl and huff when it is upset

Breeding: Apr-Aug mating; 30-40 days gestation; implantation delayed until November or December after mating

Young: 1-5 kits once every 2 years in March or April; born with eyes closed, weaned at approximately 10 weeks, stays with mother for up to a year

(more information on next page) 185

Signs: large, long cylindrical scat, tapered at one or both ends, often segmented, usually contains hair and bones

Activity: nocturnal, diurnal; alternates hunting and resting every 3-4 hours

scat

Tracks: forepaw and hind paw 4-6" (10-15 cm) long, round with well-defined pad and 5 nail marks, 5 toes on all feet; alternating fore and hind prints when walking, 4-8" (10-20 cm) stride

Stan's Notes: Extremely rare in Michigan and officially considered extirpated by the Michigan DNR. Historically found in northern Michigan, it was trapped to near extinction by the early 1900s for its rich warm fur. Since then, only a few sightings have been reported. Range includes northern Europe and Siberia and throughout northern North America, thus a wolverine in Michigan most likely came from Canada or escaped from a game farm. It is one of the least-studied large mammals in North America due to its naturally low density population. Any sighting of one of these animals should be reported to the Michigan DNR.

One of the largest members of the Weasel family. Reported to be the strongest mammal for its size. Can run with a loping gallop of about 10 miles (16 km) per hour. An excellent tree climber and strong swimmer. Like other weasels, it gives off a musky-smelling odor when threatened. Has an excellent sense of smell, but poor eyesight. This is a solitary animal that does not hibernate. Seems to enjoy snow and cold, living most of its life on the tundra or in high elevations where snow and ice rarely melt.

The genus and species names are the same and mean "glutton." Once called Glutton due to its misperceived voracious appetite; it simply eats what it can find, no more than any other animal of its size. Hunts mostly smaller animals such as rabbits and ground squirrels, but able to kill animals as large as White-tailed Deer. While it has the reputation of a ruthless killer, it feeds mainly upon winter-killed animals. Fearless, it is known for driving large predators such as bears, cougars and even lone wolves from their kills to scavenge the remains. Caches extra food and marks it with a musky scent, presumably to keep other animals away.

Will wander very long distances for extended periods of time in search of food. Male has a territory of more than 200 square miles (520 sq. km); female territory is about half the size. Long mating season compensates for its sparse distribution.

Northern River Otter
Lontra canadensis

Family: Weasels and Skunks (Mustelidae)

Size: L 2½-3½' (76-107 cm); T 11-20" (28-50 cm)

Weight: 10-30 lb. (4.5-13.5 kg)

Description: Overall dark brown-to-black fur, especially when wet, with a lighter brown-to-gray belly. Silver-to-gray chin and throat. Small ears and eyes. Short snout with white whiskers. Elongated body with a long thick tail, tapered at the tip. Male slightly larger than female.

Origin/Age: native; 7-20 years

Compare: Much larger than Mink (pg. 173) and Muskrat (pg. 81). Mink has a white patch on the chin and lacks a long thick tail. Muskrat has a long, thin naked tail.

Habitat: rivers, streams, medium to large lakes

Home: permanent and temporary dens

Food: carnivore, insectivore; fish, crayfish, frogs, small mammals, aquatic insects

Sounds: loud shrill cries when threatened, during play will grunt, growl and snort, chuckles when with mate or siblings

Breeding: Mar-Apr mating; 200-270 days gestation; implantation delayed for an unknown amount of time, entire reproduction process may take up to 1 year, female mates again days after giving birth

Young: 1-6 offspring once per year in March or April; born fully furred with eyes closed, eyes open at around 30 days, weaned at about 3 months

(more information on next page) 189

sleeping

Signs: haul outs, slides and rolling areas; scat is dark brown to green, short segments frequently contain fish bones and scales or crayfish parts, deposited on lakeshores, riverbanks, rocks or logs in water

scat

Activity: diurnal, nocturnal; active year-round, spends most of time in water, comes onto land to rest and sleep, curls up like a house cat to sleep

Tracks: hind paw 3½" (9 cm), forepaw slightly smaller, both round with well-defined heel pad and toes spread evenly apart, 5 toes on all feet; 1 set of 4 tracks when bounding; 12-24" (30-60 cm) stride

Stan's Notes: A large semi-aquatic animal that often is not very afraid of humans. Long guard hairs with a dense oily undercoat, webbed toes and streamlined body make it well suited to life in water. Special valves close the nostrils while underwater, enabling it to stay submerged for up to 6-8 minutes.

A very playful, social animal. Can be seen in small groups (mostly mothers with young), swimming and fishing in rivers and lakes. Frequently raises its head high while treading water to survey the surroundings. Enjoys sliding on belly down well-worn areas of mud, snow or ice (slides) on a riverbank or lakeshore just for fun. Can dive to depths of 50 feet (15 m). Sensitive to water pollution, quickly leaving an area that has become contaminated.

Frequently feeds on slow-moving fish such as suckers, catfish and others that are easy to catch. Mistakenly blamed for eating too many game fish. Comes to surface to eat, bringing larger items to shore to consume. Uses forepaws to manipulate, carry and tear apart food. Creates haul outs, which are well-worn trails leading from the water that often end up being littered with fish heads, scat and crayfish parts.

Likes to roll, which flattens areas of vegetation up to 6 feet (1.8 m) wide. Rolling areas have a musky odor from scent marking and usually contain some scat. Very vocal, giving a variety of sounds such as a loud whistle to communicate over long distances.

Male defends territory against other males. Female is allowed to move freely in and out of male territory. Digs its own den in a riverbank or lakeshore, often with an underwater entrance. May use an old beaver lodge. Has permanent and temporary dens. The permanent den is lined with leaves, grasses, mosses and hair and usually is where the young are born.

Becomes sexually mature at 2-3 years. A male is generally solitary except during mating season. He is not around for the birth of young, but returns in midsummer to help raise them.

Striped Skunk
Mephitis mephitis

Family: Skunks (Mephitidae)

Size: L 20-24" (50-60 cm); T 7-14" (18-36 cm)

Weight: 6-12 lb. (2.7-5.4 kg)

Description: Black with 2 broad white stripes joined at head, separated along back or upper sides and blended into sides of tail. Thin white stripe down center of head between the ears and eyes. Large, bushy black tail with a white fringe and tip. Male larger than female.

Origin/Age: native; 2-5 years

Compare: Similar size as the North American Porcupine (pg. 205), but has white stripes. Striped Skunk's bold black body and white stripes make it hard to confuse with other animals.

Habitat: woodlands, river bottoms, farmlands, woodland edges, prairies, fields, suburban and urban areas

Home: burrow, often in hollow log or tree crevice, under a deck, porch, firewood or rock pile in summer

Food: omnivore; insects, spiders, small mammals, earthworms, grubs, bird eggs, amphibians, corn, fruit, berries, nuts, seeds, reptiles

Sounds: generally quiet, will stomp front feet and exhale in a loud "pfittt," also chatters its teeth

Breeding: Feb-Apr mating; 62-66 days gestation; implantation delayed until 18-20 days after mating

Young: 4-7 offspring once per year; born naked with black and white skin (which matches the color of its future fur coat) and eyes closed, musky odor at 8-10 days, eyes open at about 24 days

(more information on next page) 193

babies in burrow juvenile

Signs: pungent odor, more obvious when the skunk has sprayed, can be detected even when it has not sprayed; cylindrical segmented scat, often dark, deposited on trails and at entrance to the den

scat

Activity: mostly nocturnal; more active during summer than winter

Tracks: hind paw 2-3½" (5-9 cm) long with 5 toes and well-defined heel pad, appearing flat-footed, forepaw 1-1¾" (2.5-4.5 cm) long and wide with 5 toes; alternating fore and hind prints are very close together when walking, 4-6" (10-15 cm) stride

Stan's Notes: Bred in the early 1900s for its fur, which explains the wide variety of colors in pet skunks today. The white stripes, which vary in length and width from one animal to another, can be used to identify individuals. Some have such wide stripes that they appear to be all white, although most are not albino.

The prominent black and white markings warn predators that it should not be approached. Will face a predator when threatened, arch its back and raise its tail while chattering its teeth. If this does not deter the predator, it will rush forward, stomp its feet, stand on forepaws with tail elevated and spray an oily, odorous yellow substance from glands at the base of its tail near the anus. Able to spray 5-6 times up to 15 feet (4.5 m) with surprising accuracy. This substance can cause temporary blindness and intense pain if it enters the eyes. Holding the animal by its tail off the ground will not prevent it from spraying.

This is a solitary, secretive skunk that wanders around in a slow, shuffling waddle in search of food. Does not hibernate, but will hole up in its burrow for several weeks to two months during cold snowy weather. Has been known to burrow in groups of up to 15 individuals, often all females. This can be a problem when the burrow is under a house because of the cumulative smell.

spraying

Genus and species names mean "bad odor" and refer to the spray.

Eastern Cottontail
Sylvilagus floridanus

Family: Rabbits and Hares (Leporidae)

Size: L 14-18" (36-45 cm); T 1-2" (2.5-5 cm)

Weight: 2-4 lb. (.9-1.8 kg)

Description: Overall gray to light brown. Black-tipped hairs give it a grizzled appearance. Usually has a small white (rarely black) spot on forehead between the ears. Large pointed ears, rarely with a black outside edge. Distinctive rusty red nape. Brown tail with a white cotton-like underside.

Origin/Age: native; 1-3 years

Compare: Slightly smaller than Snowshoe Hare (pg. 201), which usually has larger hind feet and larger ears with black tips. The Snowshoe is white in winter, while Cottontail is brown with a rusty red nape. Range can help differentiate the two in summer.

Habitat: wide variety such as suburban lawns, brush piles, rock piles, woodlands, thickets, fields

Home: small nest burrow lined with soft plant material and fur from mother's chest, covered with dry grass and leaves

Food: herbivore; grass, dandelions, other green plants in spring and summer; raspberries, roses, saplings, twigs, bark and other woody plants in winter

Sounds: loud high-pitched scream or squeal when caught by a predator such as a fox or coyote

Breeding: late Feb-Mar mating; 30 days gestation; starts to breed at 3 months

Young: 3-6 offspring up to 5 times per year; born naked and helpless with eyes closed

(more information on next page) 197

camouflaged

scat

Signs: small woody twigs and branches near the ground are cleanly cut off and at an angle, while browse from deer is higher up and has a ragged edge (due to the lack of upper incisors in deer), bark is stripped off of saplings and shrubs at the level of snow; pea-sized, round, dry, woody, light brown pellets, soft green pellets are ingested and rarely seen

Activity: nocturnal, crepuscular; often very active during late winter and early spring when males fight to breed with females

Tracks: hind paw 3-4" (7.5-10 cm) long, forepaw 1" (2.5 cm) long, small and round; 1 set of 4 tracks; forepaws fall one in front of the other behind hind prints

Stan's Notes: This is the most widespread of the eight cottontail species found in North America. Seen throughout the eastern U.S. and most of Mexico, it was transplanted to many areas that historically didn't have cottontails. Common name comes from its cotton ball-like tail.

A familiar backyard resident. Usually stays in a small area of only a couple acres. Often freezes, hunkers down and flattens ears if danger is near. Quickly runs in a zigzag pattern, circling back to its starting spot when flushed. Able to leap up to 12-15 feet (3.7-4.5 m) in a single bound while running. Also jumps sideways while running to break its scent trail. Uses a set of well-worn trails in winter, usually in thick cover of bushes. Cools itself on hot summer days by stretching out in shaded grassy areas.

Usually not a territorial animal, with fights among males breaking out only during mating season. Interspersed with chasing, males face each other, kick with front feet and jump high into the air.

After mating, female excavates a small burrow, lines it with soft plants and fur for comfort and camouflages the entrance. Mothers nurse babies at dawn and at dusk. Once the young open their eyes and are moving outside the nest burrow, they are on their own and get no further help from  their mother. One of the most reproductively successful rabbit species in North America, with some females producing as many as 35 offspring annually; however, most young do not live longer than one year.

Like other rabbits and hares, this species produces fecal pellets that are dry and brown or soft and green. Eats the green pellets to regain the nutrition that wasn't digested initially.

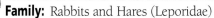

Snowshoe Hare
Lepus americanus

Family: Rabbits and Hares (Leporidae)

Size: L 15-20" (38-50 cm); T 1-2" (2.5-5 cm)

Weight: 2-3 lb. (.9-1.4 kg)

Description: Overall dark brown during summer with black-tipped hair, giving it a dark grizzled appearance. White spot on forehead between the eyes. Belly is light gray to white. Long pointed ears, black on edges. Dark brown eyes. Tail is brown above, gray or white below. Feet often yellowish. Large hind feet. White in winter with a brown nose and black-tipped white ears.

Origin/Age: native; 1-3 years

Compare: Eastern Cottontail (pg. 197) lacks the black edge on the inside of its ears, does not turn white in winter and has smaller rear feet.

Habitat: thickets, fields, swamps, boreal forests

Home: shallow nest in unmowed grassy area along fence (fencerow) or in open fields

Food: herbivore; green plants and fruit during summer, twigs, bark, coniferous needles and buds during winter, will occasionally eat carrion

Sounds: inconsequential; may give a loud squeal when captured by a large predator, will thump its large back feet on the ground when alarmed

Breeding: Mar-Jul mating; 35 days gestation

Young: 3-4 offspring 3-4 times per year; born with fur and eyes open, able to run within hours of birth; mother leaves young unattended, visits a couple times each day to nurse

(more information on next page)

winter

Signs: well-worn trails during summer, deep snow on trails in winter is packed down from frequent use; pea-sized, round with one slightly flattened side, dry, woody, light brown pellets, slightly larger than Eastern Cottontail pellets

scat

Activity: mostly nocturnal; seen during short, overcast days in deep winter

Tracks: hind paw 4-5" (10-13 cm) long and 2" (5 cm) wide, forepaw 1" (2.5 cm) long, small and round; 1 set of 4 tracks; forepaws fall one in front of the other behind hind prints

Stan's Notes: The most common "rabbit" of Michigan's North Woods. A resident of coniferous forests, living in dense thickets with ample vegetation. Ranges throughout Canada, dipping into Michigan, Wisconsin, Minnesota, the Appalachian Mountains and Rocky Mountains.

Named "Snowshoe" for its large hind feet. Extra fur grows on the hind feet in winter, enabling it to move across deep, soft snow. Has brown fur in summer, white fur in winter. Between seasons it can be patchy brown and white in color, frequently matching its environment of partially snow-covered ground. Seasonal molts are triggered by decreasing or increasing amounts of daylight.

Frequently runs in circles when chased, traveling up to 30 miles (48 km) per hour and bounding up to 14 feet (4.3 m). Often heads for thick vegetation for cover. Uses the wallows of grouse to take dust baths during summer. Usually lives a solitary life except to mate.

Although the Snowshoe Hare consumes mainly green plants, there have been reports of it eating dead animals (carrion). Populations go up and down in 10-year cycles. The causes of these fluctuations are not well understood, but most likely are tied to the abundance of food and populations of predators such as goshawks and lynx.

North American Porcupine
Erethizon dorsatum

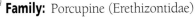

Family: Porcupine (Erethizontidae)

Size: L 20-26" (50-66 cm); T 6-12" (15-30 cm)

Weight: 7-30 lb. (3.2-13.5 kg)

Description: A short, stocky body with short legs, an arching back and quills on rump and tail. Dark brown to nearly black. Longest guard hairs are often white-tipped. Ears are small, round and barely visible. Tiny dark eyes. Small feet with long claws.

Origin/Age: native; 5-10 years

Compare: Similar size as Striped Skunk (pg. 193), but lacks white stripes. Look for the obvious body shape (arching back) and large white-tipped quills to identify. Can be seen on the ground or in trees.

Habitat: coniferous and deciduous forests, prairies, yards

Home: den in a large hollow tree or a fallen hollow log, underground burrow

Food: herbivore; soft bark, inner bark of conifers, green plants, tree leaves, leaf buds

Sounds: much vocalization with loud, shrill screeching during mating, mothers make soft grunts and groans to communicate with their babies

Breeding: Oct-Nov mating; 7 months gestation; female is receptive to mating (estrus) for only 8-12 hours; has a very long gestation period for a rodent

Young: 1 offspring once per year in May or June; born fully quilled with teeth erupted and eyes open, feeds itself within 1 week, weaned by 1 month, stays with mother until the first autumn

(more information on next page)

juvenile

Signs: large pieces of bark gnawed from conifer trunks, tooth marks on exposed wood, cleanly chewed twigs and branches laying nearby, chew marks on buildings, canoe paddles and ax handles; pile of pellets, often irregular in size and shape depending upon food intake, in summer may have segmented soft scat, hard individual pellets in winter

scat

Activity: mostly nocturnal, crepuscular; active year-round

Tracks: hind paw 3-3½" (7.5-9 cm) long, wide oval with claw marks and dotted (stippled) impression from rough, pebbled pads, forepaw 2-2½" (5-6 cm) long, oval with claw marks; 1 set of 2 tracks; fore and hind prints alternate left and right with toes pointing inward, hind paws fall near or onto fore prints, tail drag mark between each set of prints in mud or deep snow

Stan's Notes: A slow, solitary animal that is usually seen sleeping at the top of a tree or slowly crossing a road. Makes up for its slow speed by protecting itself with long, barb-tipped guard hairs that are solid at the tip and base and hollow in between. Has over 30,000 quills, which actually are modified hairs loosely attached to a sheet of muscles just beneath the skin. Unable to throw its quills, but will swing and hit with its tail, driving the tail quills deep into even the toughest flesh. Some report that quill barbs are heat sensitive and open when entering flesh, making them very hard to extract.

The sharp quills provide an excellent defense, with only very few predators capable of killing a porcupine. The Fisher is one of the few animals that is successful at flipping a porcupine over to expose its unquilled underside.

Uses a den in a large tree for sleeping during the day or for holing up for several days or weeks during cold snaps in winter. Feeds on inner bark of coniferous trees in winter, but moves to the ground to eat green vegetation in spring and summer.

Males find females during the mating season by sniffing the base of trees and rocks where a female might have passed. Males can become very aggressive toward other males, often fighting during the breeding season.

Elaborate mating with much vocalization and several males often attending one female. When the female is ready to mate, she will raise her tail to permit typical mounting.

Babies have an atypical birth, emerging headfirst with eyes open, teeth erupted and covered with quills. Quills are soft and dry and become stiff within a couple hours.

Northern Raccoon
Procyon lotor

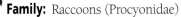

Family: Raccoons (Procyonidae)

Size: L 24-25" (60-63 cm); T 7-16" (18-40 cm)

Weight: 12-35 lb. (5.4-15.8 kg)

Description: Overall gray to brown, sometimes nearly black to silver. Distinctive black band across face (mask), eyes and down to the chin. White snout. Bushy, black-tipped brown tail with 4-6 evenly spaced dark bands or rings.

Origin/Age: native; 6-10 years

Compare: Very distinctive animal. The black mask and dark rings on the tail make it hard to confuse with any other species.

Habitat: almost all habitats from wetlands and prairies to woodlands, rural and urban

Home: hollow tree, or underground den in prairie areas

Food: omnivore; crayfish, fish, reptiles, amphibians, nuts, fruit, green leaves, suet, birdseed (especially black-oil sunflower seeds and thistle), small mammals, baby birds, bird eggs, insects

Sounds: very loud snarls, growls, hisses and screams are common (and may be frightening) during the mating season, soft purring sounds and quiet chuckles between mothers and babies

Breeding: Feb-Jun mating; 54-65 days gestation; female in heat (estrus) for only 3-6 days

Young: 3-6 offspring per year, usually in May; born with eyes closed, leaves den at 7-8 weeks

(more information on next page)

Signs: pile of half-digested berries deposited on a log, rock, under a bird feeder or on top of a garbage can; scat is usually cylindrical, 2" (5 cm) long and ¾" (2 cm) wide, but can be highly variable depending upon diet

scat

Activity: nocturnal; active year-round except during cold snaps in winter

Tracks: hind paw 3½-4½" (9-11 cm) long with 5 long toes and claw marks, forepaw 2½-3" (6-7.5 cm) long, slightly longer than wide with 5 distinct toes and claw marks; forepaws land (register) next to hind prints, 8-20" (20-50 cm) stride

Stan's Notes: Raccoons are native only to the Americas from Central America to the U.S. and lower Canada. Common name comes from the Algonquian Indian word *arougbcoune*, meaning "he scratches with his hands." Known for the ability to open such objects as doors, coolers and latches. Uses its nimble fingers to feel around the edges of ponds, rivers and lakes for crayfish and frogs. Known to occasionally wash its food before eating, hence the species name *lotor*, meaning "washer." However, it is not washing its food, but kneading and tearing it apart. The water helps it feel which parts are edible and which are not. A strong swimmer.

juveniles

Able to climb any tree very quickly and can come down headfirst or tail end first. Its nails can grip bark no matter which way it climbs because it can rotate its hind feet nearly 180 degrees so that the hind toes always point up the tree.

Active at night, sleeping in hollow trees or other dens during the day. Often mistakenly associated with forests, but also lives in prairie areas where it uses underground dens.

Usually a solitary animal as an adult. Does not hibernate but will sleep or simply hole up in a comfortable den from January to February. Will occasionally den in small groups of the same sex, usually males, or females without young.

Emerging from winter sleep, males wander many miles in search of a mate. Females use the same den for several months while raising their young, but move out afterward and find a new place to sleep each night. Males are not involved in raising young. Young remain with the adult female for nearly a year.

Virginia Opossum
Didelphis virginiana

Family: Opossums (Didelphidae)

Size: L 25-30" (63-76 cm); T 10-20" (25-50 cm)

Weight: 4-14 lb. (1.8-6.3 kg)

Description: Gray-to-brown body, sometimes nearly black. A white head, throat and belly. Long narrow snout and wide mouth. Oval, naked black ears. Long, scaly, semi-prehensile, naked pinkish tail. Short legs. Feet have 5 toes. First toe on hind feet is thumb-like and lacks a nail. Pink nose and toes.

Origin/Age: native; 3-5 years

Compare: Muskrat (pg. 81) is much smaller, all brown and rarely far from water. Norway Rat (pg. 57) also has a long naked tail, but Virginia Opossum is larger and nearly white with large dark ears and a pink nose. Norway Rat is rarely seen in trees.

Habitat: deciduous forests, farmlands, wetlands, prairies, suburban yards, cities

Home: leaf nest in an underground den or hollow log

Food: omnivore; insects, sunflower and Nyjer Thistle seeds, nuts, berries, fruit, leaves, bird eggs, fish, reptiles, amphibians, small mammals, road kill, earthworms

Sounds: low growls, hisses and shows teeth if threatened, soft clicks between mothers and young

Breeding: Jan-Feb mating; 8-14 days gestation

Young: 2-13 (usually 5-6) offspring once per year; newborns the size of a navy bean crawl to mother's external fur-lined pouch, where they attach to a nipple for as long as 2 months

(more information on next page) 213

Signs: overturned garbage cans; scat on ground under sunflower seed and Nyjer Thistle feeders

Activity: nocturnal; can be seen during the day in the coldest part of winter

scat

Tracks: hind paw 2" (5 cm) long with 5 toes, large thumb-like first toe points inward and lacks a nail, forepaw 1½" (4 cm) long with 5 toes spread out; fore and hind prints are parallel, 7" (18 cm) stride, often has a tail drag mark

Stan's Notes: This is the only marsupial found north of Mexico. Has been expanding its range in Michigan over the past 50 years. Now seen throughout the state except in the coniferous forests of northern Michigan.

A unique-looking animal, the size of a house cat. Has 50 teeth, more than any other mammal in Michigan. The tip of its naked pink tail and ears often get frostbite during winter, turn black and fall off.

Usually solitary, moving around on the ground from place to place. Also climbs trees well, using its tail to hold onto branches (semi-prehensile). While the tail is strong enough to aid in climbing, an opossum is not able to hang by its tail like a monkey.

Frequently feeds on dead animals along roads and is often hit by cars. Not a fast mover, will hiss if threatened and show its short, pointy teeth. When that doesn't work, often rolls over and feigns death with eyes closed, mouth open and tongue hanging out, "playing 'possum." Does not hibernate, but sleeps in dens for weeks during the coldest part of winter.

Males give loud, aggressive displays during the breeding season and will scent-mark by licking themselves and rubbing their heads against tree trunks or other stationary objects. Young ride on the mother's back after weaning.

Opossums can defend themselves against large predators and survive substantial injuries. One study showed nearly half of all examined dead opossums had healed broken bones, some with multiple fractures. Many opossums are immune to venomous snake bites and have a resistance to rabies and plague.

Gray Fox
Urocyon cinereoargenteus

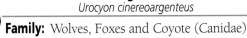

Family: Wolves, Foxes and Coyote (Canidae)

Size: L 22-24" (56-60 cm); T 10-17" (25-43 cm); H 14-15" (36-38 cm)

Weight: 7-13 lb. (3.2-5.9 kg)

Description: Grizzled gray with rusty red nape, shoulders and across the chest. Large pointed ears trimmed in white. White chin, neck and belly. Large bushy tail with a black tip and a ridge of stiff dark hairs along the top.

Origin/Age: native; 5-10 years

Compare: Less common than the Red Fox (pg. 221), which has a white-tipped tail. Coyote (pg. 225) shares the grayish appearance and black-tipped tail, but is larger than the Gray Fox and has longer legs.

Habitat: deciduous forests, rocky outcrops, river valleys, brushy areas

Home: den, mostly in a natural cavity such as a log or a crevice in rock, will enlarge a woodchuck den, unlike the den of a Red Fox, a Gray Fox den will lack a mound of dirt in front of the entrance

Food: omnivore; small mammals such as mice, moles, voles, rabbits and hares; also eats berries, apples, nuts, fish, insects and carrion

Sounds: hoarse high-pitched barks, yelps to steady high-pitched screams, mournful cries; much less vocal than the Red Fox

Breeding: winter (Jan-Mar) mating; 51-53 days gestation

Young: 1-7 kits once per year in April or May; born helpless with black fur and eyes closed

(more information on next page) 217

scat

Signs: urine and piles of feces, mostly on conspicuous landmarks such as a prominent rock, stump or trail; cylindrical scat with a tapered end, can be very dark if berries were eaten, often contains hair and bones

Activity: mostly nocturnal, crepuscular; can be seen during the day in winter, especially when overcast

Tracks: forepaw 1½" (4 cm) long, oval, hind paw slightly smaller; straight line of single tracks; hind paws fall near or directly onto fore prints (direct register) when walking, often obliterating the forepaw tracks, 10-14" (25-36 cm) stride when walking

Stan's Notes: The scientific name of the Gray Fox provides a very good description of the animal. The genus name *Urocyon* is Greek for "tailed dog." Species name *cinereoargenteus* is Latin and means "silver" or "gray and black."

Also called Treefox because it often climbs trees. Climbs to escape larger predators more than it does to find food. Sometimes it will rest in a tree. Shinnies up, pivoting its front legs at the shoulder joints to grab the trunk and pushes with hind feet. Able to rotate its front legs more than other canids. Once up the trunk, it jumps from branch to branch and has been seen up to 20 feet (6.1 m) high. Descends by backing down or running headfirst down a sloping branch.

Thought to mate for life. Male often travels 50 miles (81 km) to establish territory. A pair will defend a territory of 2-3 square miles (5-8 sq. km).

The kits are weaned at about six weeks. Male doesn't enter the den, but helps feed the family by bringing in food. Young disperse at the end of summer just before the parents start mating again.

Red Fox
Vulpes vulpes

Family: Wolves, Foxes and Coyote (Canidae)

Size: L 22-24" (56-60 cm); T 13-17" (33-43 cm); H 15-16" (38-40 cm)

Weight: 7-15 lb. (3.2-6.8 kg)

Description: Usually rusty red with dark highlights, but can vary from light yellow to black. Large pointed ears trimmed in black with white inside. White jowls, chest and belly. Legs nearly black. Large bushy tail with a white tip. Fluffy coat in winter and spring. Molts by July, appearing smaller and thinner.

Origin/Age: native, 5-10 years

Compare: Gray Fox (pg. 217) is not as red and has a black-tipped tail. Smaller than the Coyote (pg. 225), usually more red and has a white-tipped tail. All other wild canids lack a tail with a white tip.

Habitat: forests, prairies, cities, suburbs, farmlands

Home: den, usually an enlarged woodchuck den, sometimes a hollow log, may dig a den underneath a log or a rock in a bank of a stream or in a hillside created when land was cut to build a road, often has a mound of dirt up to 3 feet (1 m) high in front of the main entrance with scat deposits

Food: omnivore; small mammals such as mice, moles, voles, rabbits and hares; also eats berries, apples, nuts, fish, insects and carrion

Sounds: hoarse high-pitched barks, yelps to steady high-pitched screams, mournful cries

Breeding: Jan-Mar mating; 51-53 days gestation

Young: 1-10 kits once per year in April or May

(more information on next page) 221

summer coat

winter coat

silver morph   dark morph

scat

Signs: cylindrical scat with a tapered end, can be very dark if berries were eaten, frequently contains hair and bones, often found on a trail, prominent rock or stump or at den entrance

Activity: mainly nocturnal, crepuscular; rests during the middle of the night

Tracks: forepaw 2" (5 cm) long, oval, with hind paw slightly smaller; straight line of single tracks; hind paws fall near or directly onto fore prints (direct register) when walking, often obliterating the forepaw tracks, 10-14" (25-36 cm) stride when walking

Stan's Notes: The most widely distributed of wild canids in the world, ranging across North America, Asia, Europe and northern Africa. European Red Foxes were introduced into North America in the 1790s, resulting in some confusion regarding the original distribution and lineage.

Usually alone. Very intelligent and learns from past experiences. Often catlike in behavior, pouncing on prey. Sleeps at the base of a tree or rock, even in winter, curling itself up into a ball.

den entrance

Hunts for mice, moles and other small prey by stalking, looking and listening. Hearing differs from the other mammals. Hears low-frequency sounds, enabling it to detect small mammals digging and gnawing underground. Chases larger prey such as rabbits and squirrels. Hunts even if full, caching extra food underground or burying it in snow. Finds cached food using its memory and sense of smell.

Mated pairs will actively defend their territory from other foxes; however, they are often killed by coyotes or wolves. Uses a den only several weeks for birthing and raising young. Parents bring food to kits in the den. At first, parents regurgitate the food. Later, they will bring fresh meat and live prey to the den, allowing the kits to practice killing. Young are dispersed at the end of their first summer, with the males (dog foxes) traveling 100-150 miles (161-242 km), much farther than females (vixens), to establish their own territories.

kits

Coyote
Canis latrans

Family: Wolves, Foxes and Coyote (Canidae)

Size: L 3-3½' (1-1.1 m); T 12-15" (30-38 cm); H 2' (61 cm)

Weight: 20-40 lb. (9-18 kg)

Description: Tan fur with black and orange highlights. Large, pointed reddish orange ears with white interior. Long narrow snout with a white upper lip. Long legs and bushy black-tipped tail.

Origin/Age: native; 5-10 years

Compare: Smaller than Gray Wolf (pg. 229) with larger ears and narrower pointed snout. Red Fox (pg. 221) has black legs and a white-tipped tail.

Habitat: urban, suburban and rural areas, forests, fields, farms, highway rights-of-way

Home: den, usually in a riverbank, hillside, under a rock or tree root, entrance 1-2 feet (30-61 cm) high, can be up to 30 feet (9.1 m) deep and ends in small chamber where female gives birth; female may dig own den or enlarge a fox or badger den

Food: omnivore; small mammals, reptiles, amphibians, birds, bird eggs, insects, fruit, carrion

Sounds: barks like a dog, calls to others result in a chorus of high-pitched howling and yipping; sounds different from the lower, deeper call of the Gray Wolf, which rarely yips

Breeding: midwinter to late winter mating; 63 days average gestation

Young: 4-6 pups once per year in April or May; born with eyes closed

(more information on next page) 225

summer coat

winter coat

scat

Signs: cylindrical scat (shape is similar to that of domestic dog excrement), often containing fur and bones, along well-worn game trails, on prominent rocks and at trail intersections

Activity: nocturnal, crepuscular, diurnal; can be seen for several hours after sunrise and before sunset

Tracks: forepaw 2¼" (5.5 cm) long, round to slightly oval, hind paw slightly smaller; straight line of single tracks; hind paws fall near or directly onto fore prints (direct register) when walking, often obliterating the forepaw tracks, 12-15" (30-38 cm) stride when walking, 24-30" (60-76 cm) stride when running

Stan's Notes: Sometimes called Brush Wolf or Prairie Wolf, even though this animal is obviously not a wolf. The genus name *Canis* is Latin for "dog." The species name *latrans* is also Latin and means "barking." It is believed that the common name "Coyote" comes from the Aztec word *coyotl*, which means "barking dog."

Frequently seen as a gluttonous outlaw, this animal is only guilty of being able to survive a rapidly changing environment and outright slaughter by humans. Intelligent and playful, much like the domestic dog. Hunts alone or in small groups. Uses its large ears to hear small mammals beneath snow or vegetation. Stands over a spot, cocks its head back and forth to pinpoint prey and then pounces. Will also chase larger prey such as rabbits.

Most coyotes run with their tails down unlike dogs and wolves, which run with their tails level to upright. A fast runner, it can travel 25-30 miles (40-48 km) per hour. May even reach 40 miles (64 km) per hour for short distances. Some coyotes tracked with radio collars are known to travel more than 400 miles (644 km) over several days. Range is expanding across Michigan, except where wolves live.

Often courts for 2-3 months before mating. A monogamous animal, with mated pairs staying together for many years or for life.

Pups emerge from the den at 2-3 weeks and are weaned at 5-7 weeks. Mother will move her pups from the den when she feels threatened. Mother often gets help raising young from other group members and her mate. Pups do not return to the den once they are able to survive on their own. Mother abandons the den once the pups leave and will often return year after year in spring to use the same den.

Gray Wolf
Canis lupus

Family: Wolves, Foxes and Coyote (Canidae)

Size: L 4-5' (1.2-1.5 m); T 14-20" (36-50 cm); H 26-38" (66-96 cm)

Weight: 55-130 lb. (25-59 kg)

Description: Usually gray with dark highlights, but can vary from all white to entirely black. A large bushy tail, almost always black-tipped. Short pointed ears. Long legs. Male is slightly larger than female.

Origin/Age: native; 5-15 years

Compare: Larger than Coyote (pg. 225) and has longer legs and shorter ears. Often holds its tail straight out when traveling compared with the Coyote, which holds its tail at a downward angle.

Habitat: deciduous and coniferous forests, prairies

Home: shelter or den only for raising young, den can be 5-15 feet (1.5-4.5 m) deep, usually more than 1 entrance, fan of dirt at entrance, often scattered bones and fur laying about; used for many years

Food: omnivore; small to large mammals such as mice, rabbits, hares, deer, moose and bears; also eats berries, grass, insects and fish

Sounds: yelps, barks and howls, howling may rise and fall in pitch or remain the same; rarely has a series of yips or yelps at the end, like the Coyote

Breeding: Jan-Feb mating; 63-65 days gestation

Young: 1-10 pups once per year; born helpless with eyes closed, wide range of color variations, some look like the parents, others are completely different, remains the same color its entire life

(more information on next page)

white morph

black morph

gray morph

pups

scat

Signs: scrapes in the dirt, urine on posts, rocks and stumps; scat looks like the excrement of a domestic dog, but it is larger and contains hairs and bone fragments

Activity: nocturnal, more diurnal in winter; hunts at night in summer

Tracks: forepaw 5½-6½" (14-16 cm) long, hind paw slightly smaller, both round with clear claw marks; straight line of single tracks; hind paws fall near or directly onto fore prints (direct register) when walking, often obliterating the forepaw tracks, 15-30" (38-76 cm) stride; rarely walks along roads like a domestic dog

Stan's Notes: Largest wild dog species. Shies away from humans. Formerly ranged in the northern states, but was exterminated from most places. Now found in many areas including Michigan, Wisconsin and Minnesota.

One of the most mobile animals, traveling great distances to find food each day. Eats 3-5 pounds (1.4-2.3 kg) of meat per day, but can go weeks without food. May cache large prey items. Not a good long distance runner, but will achieve speeds of 30 miles (48 km) per hour for short distances. It is a good swimmer and will follow prey into water or swim to islands in lakes and rivers. Communicates by howling, body posturing and scent marking.

This is a social animal, living in packs of 2-15 individuals that consist primarily of family members. The pack has a well-defined hierarchy with a sole male leader called alpha and his female mate, also alpha.

Territory of a pack frequently covers 100-300 square miles (260-780 sq. km). Often uses the same well-worn trails in some areas. Territories of other packs may overlap, but conflicts rarely occur when food is plentiful.

Packs work together to hunt, chasing down prey or ambushing. Dominant members feed first. Some adults bring food back in their stomachs to pups, since mothers will not leave them for the first month. Pups will mob and lick the faces of feeder adults, encouraging regurgitation of food. When pups are older, some pack members baby-sit while the alpha pair goes hunting with the rest of the pack. Young join the pack to hunt in the fall of their first year, and leave the pack at 2-3 years to form their own or join another. After the pups leave, the pack will rendezvous before and after hunting, usually at a grassy area with a good view of the surroundings.

Bobcat
Lynx rufus

Family: Cats (Felidae)

Size: L 2¼-3½' (69-107 cm); T 3-7" (7.5-18 cm); H 2' (61 cm)

Weight: 14-30 lb. (6.3-13.5 kg)

Description: Tawny brown during summer. Light gray during winter with dark streaks and spots. Long stiff fur projects down from jowls and tapers to a point (ruffs). Triangular ears tipped with short black hairs (tufts). Prominent white spot on the back of ears. Dark horizontal barring on the upper legs. Short stubby tail with a black tip on the top and sides and a white underside. Male slightly larger than female.

Origin/Age: native; 10-15 years

Compare: Much smaller than the Cougar (pg. 241), which has a long rope-like tail. Canada Lynx (pg. 237) is larger, with long ear tufts and a black-tipped tail. Look for long ear tufts and a white underside on the tail to help identify the Bobcat.

Habitat: mixed forests, fields, wetlands, farmlands

Home: den, often in a hollow log, rock crevice or under a pile of tree branches filled with leaves

Food: carnivore; medium to small mammals such as rabbits, hares, squirrels, voles and mice; also eats birds and carrion

Sounds: raspy meows and yelps, purrs when content

Breeding: Feb-Mar mating; 60-70 days gestation

Young: 1-7 (usually 3) kittens once per year in April or May

(more information on next page) 233

scat

Signs: scratching posts with claw marks 3-4 feet (1-1.2 m) above ground, caches of larger kills covered with a light layer of leaves and twigs, scent posts marked with urine (often seen only in winter when urine sprays over on snow); long cylindrical scat, contains hair and bones, often buried, sometimes visible under a thin layer of dirt and debris

Activity: nocturnal, diurnal; often rests on hot days in a sheltered spot such as under a fallen log or in a rock crevice

Tracks: forepaw and hind paw 2" (5 cm), round, multi-lobed heel pad, 4 toes on all feet, lacking claw marks; straight line of tracks; hind paws fall near or on fore prints (direct register) when walking, often obliterating forepaw tracks, 9-13" (22.5-33 cm) stride

Stan's Notes: The most common wildcat species in Michigan. Much more common than the Canada Lynx, thriving in nearly all habitat types. The common name refers to the short, stubby or "bobbed" tail. Frequently walks with tail curled upward, which exposes the white underside, making this animal easy to identify. Makes sounds similar to a house cat.

Often uses the same trails in its territory to patrol for rabbits, which is its favorite food, and other prey. Does not climb trees as much as the Canada Lynx, but swims well. Hunts by stalking or laying in wait to attack (ambushing). Ambushes prey by rushing forward, chases and captures it, then kills it with a bite to the neck. Has been known to go without eating for several weeks during periods of famine.

Male has a larger territory than female. Usually solitary except for mating and when mothers are with young. Male will seek out a female in heat. Several males may follow a female until she is ready for mating.

Female does not breed until her second year. She has a primary (natal) den in which kittens are born and live for a short time after birth. Female also has secondary dens in her territory, where she may move her young if the natal den is disturbed. Dens are used only by the females and young. Mother raises young on her own.

kittens

Kittens are born well furred and with spots. Their eyes are closed at birth and open at about 10 days. They are weaned at approximately 8 weeks, when they start to hunt with their mother. Young stay with their mother until about 7 months, when she disperses them to mate.

Canada Lynx
Lynx canadensis

Family: Cats (Felidae)

Size: L 2½-4' (76-122 cm); T 2-5" (5-13 cm); H 2-2¼' (61-69 cm)

Weight: 20-40 lb. (9-18 kg)

Description: Light gray to brown overall. Small ears, 2" (5 cm) long, with black hairs that form a tuft. Long stiff fur projects downward from the jowls and tapers to a point (ruffs). Long legs. Large round feet. A black-tipped tail, as though dipped in ink. Male slightly larger than female.

Origin/Age: native; 10-15 years

Compare: Smaller than the Cougar (pg. 241), which has a long rope-like tail. Larger than Bobcat (pg. 233), which has short ear tufts and a white underside on the tail. Look for long ear tufts and a black-tipped tail to identify the Canada Lynx.

Habitat: coniferous forests, rocky outcrops

Home: den, usually in a hollow log, rock crevice or on leaves under a pile of tree branches; used only by female and young

Food: carnivore; medium to small mammals such as rabbits, hares, voles and mice; will also eat birds such as Ruffed Grouse and feed on carrion

Sounds: raspy meows and yelps, purrs when content, similar to a house cat

Breeding: Mar-Apr mating; 60-70 days gestation

Young: 1-5 (usually 3) kittens once per year or every 2 years; born blind and covered with spots and streaks, becomes uniformly brown at 1 year

(more information on next page)

kitten

scat

Signs: scratching posts with claw marks 3-4 feet (1-1.2 m) above ground, caches of larger kills covered with a light layer of leaves and twigs, scent posts marked with urine (often seen only in winter when urine sprays over onto snow); long cylindrical scat, contains hair and bones

Activity: nocturnal, crepuscular; often rests during the day on a tree branch or under a fallen tree or rock ledge

Tracks: forepaw and hind paw 3-4" (7.5-10 cm), round, lobed heel pad, toes spread evenly apart, lacking claw marks; straight line of tracks; hind paws fall near or directly on fore prints (direct register) when walking, often obliterating the forepaw tracks, 12-16" (30-40 cm) stride

Stan's Notes: Lives in the coniferous forests of the Upper Peninsula of Michigan. Adults are secretive and rarely seen. The young are less cautious than adults and are the ones usually seen during the day or near humans.

ear tufts

ruffs

The Canada Lynx is well suited for living in snow. It has large, round furry feet and long legs, which allow it to move quickly through deep snow. Its extra thick fur enables it to stalk silently. The extremely long ear tufts may serve as antennae by detecting vibrations. Will also hunt from trees by dropping onto prey. Can travel 5-7 miles (8-11 km) per night in search of food, mainly Snowshoe Hares and Ruffed Grouse.

Solitary except to mate and mother its young. Not afraid of water, unlike most cats.

Populations increase and decrease in 10-year cycles, depending upon the populations of the prey (predator-prey relationship). During peaks in population, ranges expand farther south. Lynx define range by scent marking key spots with urine, often on trees or shrubs near the edges of territory. The male has a larger home range than the female.

Kittens remain with the mother until about 1 year of age. Unlike adults, the young usually bury their scat.

Cougar
Puma concolor

Family: Cats (Felidae)

Size: L 5-6' (1.5-1.8 m); T 2-3' (61-91 cm); H 2½-3' (76-91 cm)

Weight: M 80-267 lb. (36-120 kg); F 64-142 lb. (29-64 kg)

Description: Overall light to tawny brown with light gray-to-white underside. White upper lip and chin, pink nose, dark spot at base of white whiskers. Small oval ears. Long legs. Large round feet. Long rope-like tail with a dark tip.

Origin/Age: native; 10-20 years

Compare: Larger than Canada Lynx (pg. 237), which has a very short tail and long black ear tufts. Bobcat is much smaller with a very short tail. Look for the long rope-like tail to identify the Cougar.

Habitat: river valleys, woodlands

Home: den, often a sheltered rock crevice, thicket, cave or other protected place; female uses den only to give birth, male does not use den

Food: carnivore; small to large mammals such as hares, rabbits, opossums, raccoons, skunks and deer

Sounds: purrs when content or with cubs, growls, snarls and hisses when threatened or in defense, loud frightening scream during mating, rarely roars

Breeding: year-round mating; 90-100 days gestation

Young: 1-6 (usually 3) cubs once every 2 years; born helpless and blind, covered with dark spots until 3 months, leaves den at 40-70 days and does not return, remains with mother until 15 months

(more information on next page)

stalking

cubs

scat

Signs: long scratches and gashes above 5 feet (1.5 m) on larger tree trunks, small piles of urine-soaked dirt and debris (serving as scent posts), caches of uneaten prey covered with small branches and leaves; large cylindrical scat up to 10" (25 cm) long and 2" (5 cm) wide, contains hair and bones, sometimes lightly covered with dirt

Activity: primarily nocturnal, to a lesser extent crepuscular; active all year, usually rests in a tree in daytime, rests near a recent kill

Tracks: forepaw and hind paw 5-6" (13-15 cm), round, lobed heel pad, toes evenly spread, lacks claw marks; straight line of tracks; hind paws fall near or onto fore prints (direct register) when walking, often obliterating the forepaw tracks, 12-28" (30-71 cm) stride

Stan's Notes: The Cougar was the most widely ranging cat in the New World in the early 1800s, from Canada to the tip of South America. It was hunted by government professionals to protect livestock from attack until the 1960s. Now seen only in scattered locations, often in remote unpopulated areas. Usually secretive and avoids humans, but has been known to attack people.

Contrary to the popular belief that it harms the deer population, it usually hunts and kills only about once each week, feeding for many days on the same kill. It hunts by stalking and springing from cover or dropping from a tree. Frequently drags its kill to a secluded area to eat, buries the carcass and returns to feed over the next couple days, often at night. It is an excellent climber and can leap distances up to 20 feet (6.1 m). Will swim if necessary.

Some people mistakenly think this cat will make a good pet and do not know what to do when their "pet" starts to knock down family members and bite them. These "pets" are released and then often turn up in suburban areas. Usually these are the animals that attack people since they have lost their fear of humans.

Home range of the male is 54-115 square miles (140-299 sq. km) and excludes other male cougars. Female range is nearly half the size of the male territory.

Solitary animal except for mating. During that time, the male accompanies the female for up to a couple weeks, traveling and sleeping with her. The female matures sexually at 2-3 years. Only the female raises the young.

male

White-tailed Deer
Odocoileus virginianus

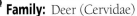

Family: Deer (Cervidae)

Size: L 4-7' (1.2-2.1 m); T 6-12" (15-30 cm); H 3-4' (1-1.2 m)

Weight: M 100-300 lb. (45-135 kg); F 75-200 lb. (34-90 kg)

Description: Reddish brown during summer, grayish brown during winter. Large ears, white inside with black edges. A white eye-ring, nose band, chin, throat and belly. Brown tail with a black tip and white underside. Male has antlers with many tines and an antler spread of 12-36" (30-90 cm). Female has a thinner neck than male and lacks antlers.

Origin/Age: native; 5-10 years

Compare: Elk (pg. 253) is over twice the size and weight of the White-tailed Deer, has a dark mane and lacks the white rump.

Habitat: all habitats

Home: no den or nest; sleeps in a different spot every night, beds may be concentrated in one area, does not use a shelter in bad weather or winter, will move to a semi-sheltered area (yard) with a good food supply in winter

Food: herbivore; grasses and other green plants, acorns and nuts in summer, twigs and buds in winter

Sounds: loud whistle-like snorts, male grunts, fawn bleats

Breeding: late Oct-Nov mating; 6-7 months gestation

Young: 1-2 fawns once per year in May or June; covered with white spots, walks within hours of birth

(more information on next page)

young male

tree rub

female

scat

Signs: browsed twigs that are ripped or torn (due to the lack of upper incisor teeth), tree rubs (saplings scraped or stripped of bark) made by male while polishing antlers during the rut, oval depressions in snow or leaves are evidence of beds; round, hard brown pellets during winter, cylindrical segmented masses of scat in spring and summer

Activity: nocturnal, crepuscular; often moves along same trails to visit feeding areas, moves around less when snow is deep

Tracks: front hoof 2-3" (5-7.5 cm) long, hind hoof slightly smaller, both with a split heart shape with a point in the front; neat line of single tracks; hind hooves fall near or directly onto fore prints (direct register) when walking

Stan's Notes: This deer is the most common large mammal in Michigan and has the most widespread range. Originally was not found throughout the state. Its range expanded dramatically in the mid- to late 1800s due to logging and overhunting of native elk; now found in nearly every habitat in every part of Michigan. Also known as Virginia Deer or Whitetail.

fawn

Much longer guard hairs in winter give the animal a larger appearance than in summer. Individual hairs of the winter coat are thick and hollow and provide excellent insulation. Falling snow often does not melt on its back.

In summer, antlers are covered with a furry skin called velvet. Velvet contains a network of blood vessels that supplies nutrients to the growing antlers. New antler growth begins after the male (buck) drops his antlers in January or February. Some females (does) have been known to grow antlers.

Deer are dependent on the location of the food supply. In winter large groups move to low moist areas (yards) that have plenty of white cedar trees. This yarding behavior helps keep trails open and provides some protection from predators. Eats 5-9 pounds (2.3-4.1 kg) of food per day, preferring acorns in fall and fresh grass in spring. Its four-chambered stomach enables the animal to get nutrients from poor food sources such as twigs and eat and drink substances that are unsuitable for humans.

Able to run up to 37 miles (60 km) per hour, jump up to 8½ feet (2.6 m) high and leap 30 feet (9.1 m). Also an excellent swimmer.

The buck is solitary in spring and early summer, but seeks other bucks in late summer and early fall to spar. Bucks are polyga-mous. The largest, most dominant bucks mate with many does.

For a couple weeks after birth, fawns lay still all day while their mother is away feeding. Mother nurses them evenings and nights.

male

Moose
Alces alces

Family: Deer (Cervidae)

Size: L 7-9' (2.1-2.7 m); T 4-7" (10-18 cm); H 6½-7½' (2-2.3 m)

Weight: M 900-1,400 lb. (405-630 kg); F 700-1,100 lb. (315-495 kg)

Description: Dark reddish brown fur, lighter brown in winter. Large light brown ears. Bulbous muzzle, usually darker than head. Obvious hump at shoulders. Nearly black belly and legs. Small brown tail. Male has a flap of skin hanging underneath the chin (dewlap), flattened (palmate) antlers with multiple points and an antler spread of 4-5' (1.2-1.5 m). Female is much smaller than male and lacks the dewlap and antlers.

Origin/Age: native; 15-20 years

Compare: Hard to misidentify this extremely large animal.

Habitat: mixed forests, coniferous forests, wetlands

Home: no den or nest; will bed in a different spot each night, beds may be concentrated in one area, will move to a semi-sheltered area (yard) with a good food supply during winter

Food: herbivore; aquatic vegetation, grasses and other green plants, acorns, nuts, twigs, buds

Sounds: during the rut, male bellows loudly, grunts and groans, female gives long moans

Breeding: late Sep-Nov mating; 8 months gestation

Young: 1-2 (usually 1) calves in spring; light brown fur, lacks spots, stands and walks within 24 hours, swims at about 7 days

(more information on next page) 249

flehmening

shedding velvet

tree rub

mother and calf

summer scat

winter scat

Signs: tree rubs (saplings scraped or stripped of bark), made by the male while polishing antlers during the rut, browsed twigs that are ripped or torn, depressions in the ground (scrapes) up to 4 feet (1.2 m) wide, often muddy with a strong smell of urine; cylindrical segmented masses of scat in spring and summer, frequently green to nearly black, large brown pellets in winter, usually round and hard

Activity: nocturnal, crepuscular

Tracks: front hoof 5-6" (13-15 cm) long, hind hoof slightly smaller, both with a split heart shape with a point in the front; line of individual tracks; hind hooves fall near or to side of fore prints; heart shape widens and 2 dots (made by dewclaws) print just behind each heart-shaped print when in mud or snow

Stan's Notes: Only one moose species worldwide, with several subspecies. Found in cooler regions due to its stomach (which produces heat by fermentation), its inability to perspire and its large size. The common name comes from the native Algonquian Indian word *moos*, which refers to its habit of eating twigs.

The function of the flap of skin under the male's neck (dewlap) is unknown. Poor vision, but excellent hearing and the ability to smell food underneath snow. Has a four-chambered stomach for processing woody plants. Able to eat up to 45 pounds (20.3 kg) of vegetation per day. An extremely quiet animal while feeding in the woods. May appear slow and gangly, but can run up to 35 miles (56 km) per hour and swim up to 6 miles (10 km) per hour for long periods. Spends much time in the water, eating aquatic plants, taking refuge from biting insects and heat.

The male (bull) is solitary in summer and seeks breeding females (cows) in fall. Matures sexually before 5-7 years, but is not large enough to compete with dominant bulls for cows until after 5-7 years. Reaches prime condition at 7-12 years. Visually attuned to an opponent's antlers, it will spar with other bulls, usually those with a similar antler size, to assert dominance and to determine which will mate with available cows. Often seen curling its upper lip back while extending its neck (flehmening) when around cows. The lip curl is thought to enhance the sense of smell and allow the bull to detect when a cow is in estrus. Cows group together in winter where food is available and snow is packed down, which makes walking easier.

A wandering moose will often make the local news when sighted in urban areas. This behavior often is the result of a fatal disorder caused by a worm in the brain, prevalent (endemic) in White-tailed Deer. An afflicted moose will wander in a straight line for hundreds of miles.

male

Elk
Cervus canadensis

Family: Deer (Cervidae)

Size: L 7-9½' (2.1-2.9 m); T 3-8" (7.5-20 cm); H 4½-5' (1.4-1.5 m)

Weight: M 600-1,100 lb. (270-495 kg); F 450-650 lb. (203-293 kg)

Description: Brown to tan with a darker head, neck, belly and legs. Rump patch is light tan to yellowish. Short stubby tail. Male has large antlers with many tines and an antler spread of 4-5' (1.2-1.5 m). Female has a lighter mane than male, a thinner neck and lacks antlers.

Origin/Age: native; 15-20 years

Compare: Smaller than Moose (pg. 249), which is darker brown and lacks a light rump patch. More than twice the size and weight of its cousin, the White-tailed Deer (pg. 245), which lacks the dark mane.

Habitat: mixed forests, fields, farmlands, prairie

Home: no den or nest; rests out in the open on the ground, will bed in a different area each night

Food: herbivore; grasses and other green plants

Sounds: snorts and grunts, male gives a bugle call or high-pitched whistle to challenge other males during rut; call can be heard up to several miles away

Breeding: late Aug-Nov mating; 9 months gestation

Young: 1-2 calves once per year in June or July; covered with spots until about 3 months, feeds solely by nursing for the first 30 days, weaned at 9 months

(more information on next page) 253

bugling

sparring

female

Signs: tree rubs (saplings scraped or stripped of bark) made by the male while polishing antlers during rut, ground scrapes (shallow depressions in the ground) made by male hooves to attract females and where male urinates and defecates, shallow depressions in snow made from resting

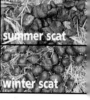

summer scat

winter scat

Activity: nocturnal, crepuscular; can be seen during the day walking and feeding

Tracks: front hoof 4-4½" (10-11 cm) long, hind hoof slightly smaller, both with a split heart shape with a point in the front; line of individual tracks; hind hooves fall near or onto fore prints (direct register) when walking, often obliterating the front hoof tracks; heart shape widens and 2 dots (made by dewclaws) print just behind each heart-shaped print when in mud or snow

Stan's Notes: There is only one species of elk in North America, but there are four subspecies. Sometimes called Wapiti, which is a Shawnee Indian word meaning "pale deer." The British name for the moose is "Elk." This name apparently was misapplied by our early settlers and has remained since.

Once widespread in the prairie and hardwood regions of western Michigan, but now seen only in a couple of areas in the state. Elk disappeared from Michigan by 1875. All current elk in Michigan have come from releases in 1918, when seven individuals were released near Wolverine. Small herds were reintroduced in 1918 into one location, where herds can still be found today.

A highly gregarious animal. Most herds consist of many females (cows) and calves. While herds in western states are composed of as many as several hundred individuals, Michigan herds are smaller. Highly territorial, marking edges of its area with a scent secreted from glands on the sides of its chin and muzzle. Makes a shallow, saucer-like depression in the dirt (wallow) in which it rolls, coating its fur with dust to help protect against annoying insects. It is a fast animal, with bulls capable of reaching 35 miles (56 km) per hour for short distances. Also a strong swimmer that will wade across nearly any river or stream.

A bull is solitary or found in small groups, but will join the herd during the rut. Bulls are capable of breeding at 2 years. However, rarely is a bull large enough at that age to fight off older males and establish a harem. Will thrash small trees to polish its antlers. Tears up vegetation and wears it on antlers to express dominance. Top bulls challenge each other by clashing their antlers together in a jousting fashion. Rarely do these fights result in any injury or death. The most polygamous animal in America, one bull will mate with all cows in the harem.

The cow becomes sexually mature at 3 years. Cow will leave the herd to give birth, rejoining the group 4-10 days later.

Black Bear
Ursus americanus

Family: Bears (Ursidae)

Size: L 4½-6' (1.4-1.8 m); T 3-7" (7.5-18 cm); H 3-3½' (1-1.1 m)

Weight: M 100-900 lb. (45-405 kg); F 90-525 lb. (41-236 kg)

Description: Nearly all black, sometimes brown, tan or cinnamon. Short round ears. Light brown snout. May have a small white patch on its chest. Short tail, which often goes unnoticed.

Origin/Age: native; 5-30 years

Compare: The only bear species in Michigan.

Habitat: forests, wetlands, prairies, farmlands

Home: den, beneath a fallen tree or in a rock crevice or cave, may dig a den 5-6 feet (1.5-1.8 m) deep with a small cavity at the end; male sometimes hibernates on the ground without shelter instead of using a den

Food: omnivore; leaves, nuts, roots, fruit, berries, grass, insects, fish, small mammals, carrion

Sounds: huffs and puffs or grunts and groans when walking, loud snorts made by air forced from nostrils, loud roars when fighting and occasionally when mating, a motor-like hum when content

Breeding: Jun-Jul mating, female mates every other year; 60-90 days gestation; implantation delayed until November after mating

Young: 1-5 (often 2) cubs in January or February; ½-1 lb. (.2-.5 kg), covered with fine dark fur

(more information on next page) 257

claw marks

brown morph

scat

Signs: series of long narrow scars on tree trunks, usually as high as the bear can reach, made by scratching and biting, rub marks with snagged hair on the lower part of tree trunks or on large rocks, made by rubbing and scratching when shedding its winter coat; large dark cylindrical scat or piles of loose scat, usually contains berries and nuts, may contain animal hair, undigested plant stems and roots

Activity: primarily nocturnal; often seen feeding during the day

Tracks: hind paw 7-9" (18-22.5 cm) long, 5" (13 cm) wide with 5 toes, turns inward slightly, looks like a human track, forepaw 4" (10 cm) long, 5" (13 cm) wide with 5 toes, claw marks on all feet; fore and hind prints are parallel, hind paws fall several inches in front of fore prints; shuffles feet when walking

Stan's Notes: The Black Bear is unique to North America. Has a shuffling gait and frequently appears clumsy. It is not designed for speed, but can run up to 30 miles (48 km) per hour for short distances. A powerful swimmer, however, and good at climbing trees. It has color vision, but poor eyesight and relies on smell to find most of its food. Often solitary except for mating in early summer or when bears gather at a large food supply such as a garbage dump. Feeds heavily throughout the summer, adding layers of fat for hibernation.

Hibernates up to six months per year beginning in late fall. Heart rate drops from 70 to 10-20 beats per minute. Body temperature drops only 1-12°F (-17°C to -11°C), which is not enough to change mental functions. Doesn't eat, drink, pass feces or urinate during hibernation, yet can be roused and will move around in the den. The female can lose up to 40 percent of her body weight during hibernation.

cub

Male has a large territory of up to 15 square miles (39 sq. km) that often encompasses several female territories. Males fight each other for breeding rights and usually have scars from fights. The male bear matures at 3-4 years of age, but doesn't reach full size until 10-12 years. Males do not take part in raising young.

The female bear doesn't breed until it is 2-3 years of age. Females that have more body fat when entering hibernation will have more cubs than females with less fat. If a female does not have enough fat, she will not give birth. Mother bears, which average 177 pounds (80 kg), are approximately 250 times the size of newborns. A short gestation and tiny cubs are the result of the reproductive process during hibernation.

male

American Bison
Bison bison

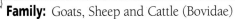

Family: Goats, Sheep and Cattle (Bovidae)

Size: L 8-12' (2.4-3.6 m); T 12-19" (30-48 cm); H 5-6' (1.5-1.8 m)

Weight: M 1,000-2,000 lb. (450-900 kg); F 800-1,000 lb. (360-450 kg)

Description: Dark brown head, lighter brown body and large humped shoulders. Bearded with a long shaggy mane over head and shoulders. Long tuft-tipped tail. Both sexes have short curved horns, which are not shed.

Origin/Age: native; 20-25 years

Compare: A massive animal, hard to confuse with any other. No longer roams freely in Michigan. Rarely seen beyond established areas in parks and farms.

Habitat: prairies, farmlands, open forests

Home: does not use a den or nest, even in bad weather or winter; beds in a different spot each night, rests in the open, laying on the ground or in snow during winter

Food: herbivore; grasses and other green plants, lichens

Sounds: often quiet; male bellows during the rut, female snorts, young bawls for mother's attention

Breeding: Jul-Aug mating; 9-10 months gestation

Young: 1 calf every 1-2 years in May or June; born with reddish brown fur, stands within 30 minutes, walks within hours of its birth, joins herd at 2-3 days, acquires hump, horns and adult coloration at 2-3 months, weaned at 6-7 months

(more information on next page)

flehmening

female

scat

Signs: saucer-like depressions in dirt (wallows), 8-10 feet (2.4-3 m) wide, trees and shrubs with the bark rubbed off, shallow depressions in the snow are evidence of bison beds; scat is similar to that of the domestic cow, flat round patties, 12-14 inches (30-36 cm) wide

Activity: crepuscular; often rests in daytime to chew its cud

Tracks: front hoof 6-7" (15-18 cm) long, hind hoof slightly smaller, both with opposing crescents and more pointed in the front; hind hooves fall behind and slightly to the side of fore prints; crescents widen when walking in mud or running

Stan's Notes: Although considered extirpated in the state (locally extinct), today some bison exist in Michigan in managed herds. The largest land mammal in North America and considered iconic to the New World. Sometimes called Buffalo, but not related to the Old World buffalo. It once numbered in the tens of millions and was hunted to near extinction around 1830, when a government policy advocated extermination. There were no bison left in Michigan by 1880. By the early 1900s, fewer than 1,000 bison remained in the U.S. Population restoration started shortly thereafter.

Before it was nearly eliminated, great herds would migrate long distances between winter and summer grounds. Seen today in many parts of the U.S., but it is no longer migratory. A gregarious animal, gathering in large herds of nearly 100 individuals, mainly females (cows) and calves.

Uses its massive head and extremely powerful neck muscles to push aside deep snow in winter to feed upon the brown grass below. Rolls and rubs its body in wallows to relieve insect bites.

The male (bull) is usually on its own or in a small group during autumn and winter. A dominant bull will join a maternal herd late in summer, just before the rut. Cows 2-3 years and older have reached sexual maturity and are fertile for only about 24 hours. Bulls curl their upper lip and extend the neck (flehmening) when around cows, perhaps to detect estrus. A bull "tends" cows in estrus rather than maintaining harems. Competing bulls strut near each other, showing off their profile. Mature bulls will face each other, charge, crash headfirst and use their massive necks to push each other. Fights rarely result in injury, but occasionally hooking or goring occurs.

sparring

GLOSSARY

Browse: Twigs, buds and leaves that deer, moose, elk and other animals eat.

Canid: A member of the Wolves, Foxes and Coyote family, which includes dogs.

Carnivore: An animal such as a mink, fox or wolf that eats the flesh of other animals for its main nutrition.

Carrion: Dead or decaying flesh. Carrion is a significant food source for many animal species.

Cecum: The large pouch that forms the beginning of the large intestine. Also known as the blind gut.

Cheek ruff: A gathering of long stiff hairs on each side of the face of an animal, ending in a downward point. Seen in bobcats and lynx.

Coprophagy: The act of reingesting fecal pellets. Coprophagy enables rabbits and hares to gain more nourishment since the pellets pass through the digestive system a second time.

Crepuscular: Active during the early morning and late evening hours as opposed to day or night. See *diurnal* and *nocturnal*.

Cud: Food regurgitated from the first stomach to the mouth, and chewed again. Cud is produced by hoofed animals such as deer or bison, which have a four-chambered stomach (ruminants).

Dewclaw: A non-functional (vestigial) digit on the feet of some animals, which does not touch the ground. Seen in deer, elk and moose.

Dewlap: A fold of loose skin hanging from the neck of some animals such as moose.

Direct register: The act of a hind paw landing or registering in the track left by a forepaw, resulting in two prints that appear like one track. Usually occurs when walking.

Diurnal: Active during daylight hours as opposed to nighttime hours. Opposite of *nocturnal*.

Drey: The nest of a squirrel.

Duff: The layer of decaying leaves, grasses, twigs or branches, often several inches thick, on a forest floor or prairie.

Echolocation: A sensory system in bats, dolphins and some shrews, in which inaudible, high-pitched sounds are emitted and the returning echoes are interpreted to determine the direction and distance of objects such as prey.

Estrus: A state of sexual readiness in most female animals that immediately precedes ovulation, and the time when females are most receptive to mating. Also known as heat.

Extirpate: To hunt or trap into extinction in a region or state.

Flehmen: The lift of the upper lip and grimace an animal makes when it draws air into its mouth and over its Jacobson's organ, which is thought to help analyze the scents (pheromones) wafting in the air. Frequently seen in cats, deer and bison.

Fossorial: Well suited for burrowing or digging. Describes an animal such as a mole.

Gestation: Pregnancy. The period of development in the uterus of a mammal from conception up to birth.

Grizzled: Streaked or tipped with gray, or partly gray. Describes the appearance of some fur.

Guard hairs: The long outer hairs of an animal's coat, which provide warmth. Guard hairs are typically hollow and usually thicker and darker than the soft hairs underneath.

Haul out: A well-worn trail or area on the shore where an animal such as an otter climbs or hauls itself out of the water.

Herbivore: An animal such as a rabbit, deer, moose or elk that eats plants for its main nutrition.

Hibernation: A torpid or lethargic state characterized by decreased heart rate, respiration and body temperature, and occurring in close quarters for long periods during winter. See *torpor*.

Hoary: Partly white or silver streaked, or tipped with white or silver. Describes the appearance of some fur.

Hummock: A low mound or ridge of earth or plants.

Insectivore: An animal such as a shrew that eats insects as its main nutrition.

Keratin: A hard protein that is the chief component of the hair, nails, horns and hooves of an animal.

Microflora: Bacterial life living in the gut or first stomach of an animal. Microflora help break down food and aid in the digestive process.

Midden: A mound or deposit of pine cone parts and other refuse. A midden is evidence of a favorite feeding site of an animal such as a squirrel.

Morph: One of various distinct shapes, structural differences or colors of an animal. Color morphs do not change during the life of an animal.

Nictitating membrane: A second, inner eyelid, usually translucent, that protects and moistens the eye.

Nocturnal: Active during nighttime hours as opposed to daylight hours. Opposite of *diurnal*.

Nonretractile: That which cannot be drawn back or in. Describes the claws of a dog. Opposite of *retractile*.

Omnivore: An animal such as a bear that eats a wide range of foods including plants, insects and the flesh of other animals as its main nutrition.

Patagium: A thin membrane extending from the body to the front and hind limbs, forming a wing-like extension. Seen in flying squirrels and bats.

Population: All individuals of a species within a specific area.

Predator: An animal that hunts, kills and eats other animals. See *prey*.

Prey: An animal that is hunted, killed and eaten by a predator. See *predator*.

Retractile: That which can be drawn back or in. Describes the claws of a cat. Opposite of *nonretractile*.

Rut: An annually recurring condition of sexual readiness and reproductive activity in mammals such as deer and elk that usually occurs in autumn. See *estrus*.

Scat: The fecal droppings of an animal.

Scent marking: A means of marking territory, signaling sexual availability or communicating an individual's identity. An animal scent marks with urine, feces or by secreting a tiny amount of odorous liquid from a gland, usually near the base of the tail, chin or feet, onto specific areas such as rocks, trees and stumps.

Semi-prehensile: Suited for partially seizing, grasping or holding, especially by wrapping around an object, but not a means of full support. Describes the tail of an opossum.

Stride: In larger animals, the distance between individual tracks. In smaller animals such as weasels, the distance between sets of tracks.

Subnivean: Below the surface of snow, but above the surface of the earth. See *subterranean*.

Subterranean: Below the surface of the earth.

Tannin: A bitter-tasting astringent found in the nuts of many plant species.

Torpor: A torpid or lethargic state resembling hibernation, characterized by decreased heart rate, respiration and body temperature, but usually shorter, lasting from a few hours to several days or weeks. See *hibernation*.

Tragus: A fleshy projection in the central part of the ear of most bats. The size and shape of the tragus may be used to help identify some bat species.

Tree rub: An area on small to medium trees where the bark has been scraped or stripped off. A tree rub is made by a male deer polishing his antlers in preparation for the rut.

Velvet: A soft furry covering on antlers, which contains many blood vessels that support antler growth. Velvet is shed when antlers reach full size. Seen in the Deer family.

Vibrissae: Sensitive bristles and hairs such as whiskers that help an animal feel its way in the dark. Vibrissae are often on the face, legs and tail.

Wallow: A depression in the ground that is devoid of vegetation, where an animal such as a bison rolls around on its back to "bathe" in dirt.

HELPFUL RESOURCES

Emergency

For an animal bite, please seek medical attention at an emergency room or call 911. Injured or orphaned animals should be turned over to a licensed wildlife rehabilitator. Check your local listings for a rehabilitator near you.

Web Pages

The internet is a valuable place to learn more about mammals. You may find studying mammals on the net a fun way to discover additional information about them or to spend a long winter night. These websites will assist you in your pursuit of mammals. If a web address doesn't work (they often change a bit), just enter the name of the group into a search engine to track down the new web address.

Site and Address:

Smithsonian Institution - North American Mammals
www.mnh.si.edu/mna

The American Society of Mammalogists
www.mammalsociety.org

National Wildlife Rehabilitators Association
www.nwrawildlife.org

International Wildlife Rehabilitation Council
www.theiwrc.org

Michigan DNR
www.michigan.gov/dnr

Author Stan Tekiela's home page
www.naturesmart.com

Michigan's Artiodactyla Order

ORDER	SUBORDER	FAMILY	SUBFAMILY

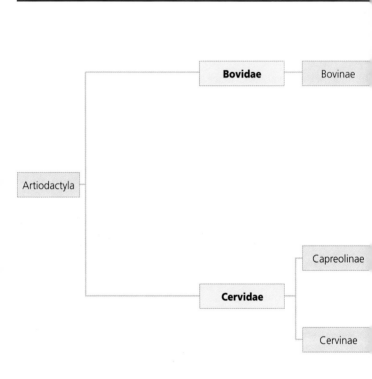

American Bison pg. 261
Bison bison

White-tailed Deer pg. 245
Odocoileus virginianus

Moose pg. 249
Alces alces

Elk pg. 253
Cervus canadensis

Box colors match the
corresponding section of the book.

Michigan's Carnivora Order

| ORDER | SUBORDER | FAMILY | SUBFAMILY |

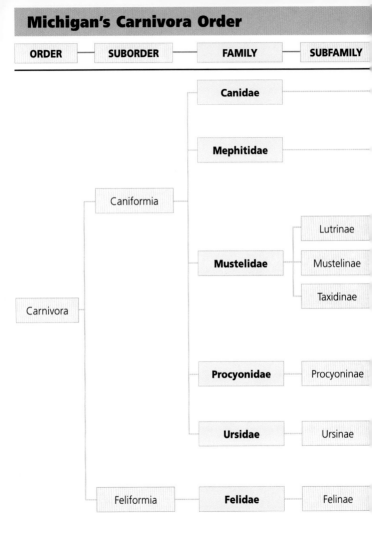

Gray Fox pg. 217
Urocyon cinereoargenteus

Red Fox pg. 221
Vulpes vulpes

Coyote pg. 225
Canis latrans
Gray Wolf pg. 229
Canis lupus

Striped Skunk pg. 193
Mephitis mephitis

Northern River Otter pg. 189
Lontra canadensis

Least Weasel pg. 157
Mustela nivalis
Short-tailed Weasel pg. 161
Mustela erminea
Long-tailed Weasel pg. 165
Mustela frenata

American Marten pg. 169
Martes americana
Fisher pg. 177
Martes pennanti

Mink pg. 173
Neovison vison

Wolverine pg. 185
Gulo gulo

Northern Raccoon pg. 209
Procyon lotor

American Badger pg. 181
Taxidea taxus

Black Bear pg. 257
Ursus americanus

Bobcat pg. 233
Lynx rufus
Canada Lynx pg. 237
Lynx canadensis

Cougar pg. 241
Puma concolor

Box colors match the
corresponding section of the book.

Michigan's Chiroptera Order

ORDER	SUBORDER	FAMILY	SUBFAMILY

| Chiroptera | Microchiroptera | **Vespertilionidae** | Vespertilioninae |

Michigan's Didelphimorphia Order

ORDER	SUBORDER	FAMILY	SUBFAMILY

| Didelphimorphia | | **Didelphidae** | Didelphinae |

Marsupial

Box colors match the
corresponding section of the book.

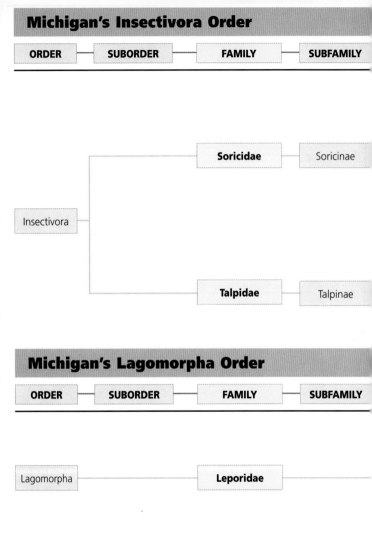

Michigan's Insectivora Order

ORDER	SUBORDER	FAMILY	SUBFAMILY

Insectivora

Soricidae — Soricinae

Talpidae — Talpinae

Michigan's Lagomorpha Order

ORDER	SUBORDER	FAMILY	SUBFAMILY

Lagomorpha — **Leporidae**

Shrews and Moles

Least Shrew pg. 5
Cryptotis parva

Masked Shrew pg. 9
Sorex cinereus

Pygmy Shrew pg. 13
Sorex hoyi

Arctic Shrew pg. 21
Sorex arcticus

Water Shrew pg. 25
Sorex palustris

Northern Short-tailed Shrew pg. 17
Blarina brevicauda

Star-nosed Mole pg. 29
Condylura cristata

Eastern Mole pg. 33
Scalopus aquaticus

Rabbit and Hares

Eastern Cottontail pg. 197
Sylvilagus floridanus

Snowshoe Hare pg. 201
Lepus americanus

Box colors match the
corresponding section of the book.

Michigan's Rodentia Order

ORDER	SUBORDER	FAMILY	SUBFAMILY

Rodentia

- Castorimorpha — **Castoridae**
- Hystricomorpha — **Erethizontidae**
- Myomorpha
  - **Dipodidae** — Zapodinae
  - **Muridae**
    - Arvicolinae
    - Murinae
    - Sigmodontinae
- Sciuromorpha — **Sciuridae**
  - Sciurinae
  - Xerinae

Rodents

American Beaver pg. 85
Castor canadensis

North American Porcupine pg. 205
Erethizon dorsatum

Meadow Jumping Mouse pg. 37
Zapus hudsonius

Woodland Jumping Mouse pg. 41
Napaeozapus insignis

Southern Red-backed Vole pg. 61
Clethrionomys gapperi

Woodland Vole pg. 65
Microtus pinetorum
Meadow Vole pg. 69
Microtus pennsylvanicus
Prairie Vole pg. 73
Microtus ochrogaster

Southern Bog Lemming pg. 77
Synaptomys cooperi

Muskrat pg. 81
Ondatra zibethicus

House Mouse pg. 45
Mus musculus

Norway Rat pg. 57
Rattus norvegicus

White-footed Mouse pg. 49
Peromyscus leucopus
Deer Mouse pg. 53
Peromyscus maniculatus

Northern Flying Squirrel pg. 133
Glaucomys sabrinus
Southern Flying Squirrel pg. 133
Glaucomys volans

Red Squirrel pg. 141
Tamiasciurus hudsonicus

Eastern Gray Squirrel pg. 145
Sciurus carolinensis
Eastern Fox Squirrel pg. 149
Sciurus niger

Least Chipmunk pg. 125
Tamias minimus
Eastern Chipmunk pg. 129
Tamias striatus

Thirteen-lined Ground Squirrel pg. 137
Ictidomys tridecemlineatus

Woodchuck pg. 153
Marmota monax

Box colors match the
corresponding section of the book.

CHECKLIST/INDEX BY SPECIES

Use the boxes to check the mammals you've seen.

ABOUT THE AUTHOR

Naturalist, wildlife photographer and writer Stan Tekiela is the originator of the popular state-specific field guide series that includes *Birds of Michigan Field Guide*. Stan has authored more than 190 educational books, including field guides, quick guides, nature books, children's books, playing cards and more, presenting many species of animals and plants.

With a Bachelor of Science degree in Natural History from the University of Minnesota and as an active professional naturalist for more than 30 years, Stan studies and photographs wildlife throughout the United States and Canada. He has received various national and regional awards for his books and photographs. Also a well-known columnist and radio personality, his syndicated column appears in more than 25 newspapers, and his wildlife programs are broadcast on a number of Midwest radio stations. Stan can be followed on Facebook and Twitter. He can be contacted via www.naturesmart.com.